THE NEW HUMANITY SHIFT

Generation Alpha Reshaping Society

Written By

Soren Fielding and Nicholas J. Matyas

"Every generation inherits the same sunrise. Only its eyes decide how brightly it shines." - Santiago Dagon

The Discovery Walkabout Collection Of

Reflective Writings

Legal Information and Disclaimer

This book contains references to studies, organizations, companies, platforms, publications, and quotations believed to be accurate at the time of writing. The author has made a good faith effort to present information that is factual, fair, and balanced.

Some material in this book reflects analysis, interpretation, opinion, or observation. These viewpoints may be based on the author's personal experiences, on experiences shared by others, or on publicly available research and reporting. Such perspectives are offered for informational and educational purposes and should not be construed as statements of fact about any individual or entity.

The inclusion or mention of any organization, company, platform, or study does not imply endorsement, criticism, or wrongdoing unless explicitly stated. All trademarks and names are the property of their respective owners.

Despite careful research and review, errors or omissions may occur. If a factual discrepancy is identified, the authors and publisher are committed to addressing it promptly and fairly. Where appropriate, corrections or clarifications will be issued in future editions or public updates.

Nothing in this book is intended as legal, financial, or professional advice. Readers are encouraged to verify information independently and to exercise their own judgment when interpreting the material presented.

INTRODUCTION

The future often feels as though it belongs somewhere ahead of us. When attention slows, it becomes clear that it is already here. It shows itself in ordinary moments. In how children interact with technology before they learn to explain it. In how they sense connection long before they understand structure. In how they navigate complexity without treating it as unusual.

Generation Alpha is growing up within a world shaped by constant connection. Digital networks form the background of daily life, not as tools added on, but as conditions already present. Because of this, their way of relating to people, information, and authority does not follow earlier patterns exactly. It suggests the beginning of a New Humanity Shift, one that reaches beyond technology and into how leadership, responsibility, and purpose are understood.

The New Humanity Shift does not announce itself through disruption alone. It unfolds through changes in attention, expectation, and emotional awareness. Leadership within this New Humanity Shift appears less centered on control and more on coherence. Influence becomes linked to trust, clarity, and the capacity to remain grounded while complexity increases. Generation Alpha is not preparing to lead within old structures alone. They are forming inside a moment when those structures are already changing.

"The morning does not arrive because something new appears. It arrives because we learn how to look again."
- Santiago Dagon

Generation Alpha is entering a world filled with possibility and uncertainty at the same time. They are learning early how opportunity and responsibility exist together. They sense quickly when systems feel misaligned, and they tend to respond more to coherence than command.

Their contribution is unlikely to be defined by technical ability alone. It may emerge through emotional understanding, ethical awareness, and the capacity to hold multiple perspectives without collapse. These qualities have always shaped effective leadership. What changes now is how early they begin to matter.

The year 2026 marks an important threshold. The oldest members of Generation Alpha move into adolescence; a stage long associated with identity formation and moral awareness. How they experience these years may influence not only personal development, but how education, work, and leadership continue to evolve. Their expectations may gently challenge institutions shaped for earlier conditions.

For those who came before them, the role is not to manage every outcome. It is to remain attentive. To ask questions alongside them. To help make sense of change rather than resist it reflexively. Leadership in this moment often looks less like direction and more like accompaniment.

Technology will continue to expand possibilities. It will not replace responsibility. Tools still reflect intention. Systems still amplify values. Connection still depends on understanding.

"The wise are not troubled by what approaches. They step forward carrying the strength they have always held."
- Santiago Dagon

This book joins an ongoing conversation between generations. It does not stand apart from it. To read these pages is to stand in that shared space between what has been learned and what is still forming.

As you read the chapters ahead, take time to pause when something catches your attention. Let questions remain open instead of rushing to conclusions. This book is meant to encourage deeper thinking and new perspectives, not to predict outcomes or pass judgment. If you finish with even one new insight, the book has fulfilled its purpose.

This book uses a different approach to structure. Instead of long chapters, each chapter is divided into short sections. These sections are designed to help readers pause and think more deeply. Each chapter and each section can stand on its own, while also contributing to the larger perspective of the New Humanity Shift. Repetition and restated ideas are included on purpose to support focus, clarity, and understanding. Some ideas are left open rather than fully resolved, encouraging reflection, questions, and moments of pause instead of quick conclusions.

What follows is a series of observations and brief explorations. Each theme offers a glimpse into how society may unfold within a culture shaped by rapid change and continuous connection. Notice what resonates with your own experience. Observe how these patterns appear in the children and young people around you. The intention is not to forecast outcomes, but to examine how life appears to be shifting, and what that New Humanity Shift may suggest for the years ahead.

The story of Generation Alpha is part of our own story. It continues the long unfolding of humanity. Progress has never depended only on speed. It has always depended on how clearly people understand where they stand and why they are moving forward.

"Every child born in Generation Alpha carries an inner compass. Our task is not to direct their steps, but to help them trust the direction already within them."

- *Santiago Dagon*

The journey begins here, with the understanding that the future is already taking shape. It is unfolding through Generation Alpha, influencing leadership and society through awareness rather than force, one moment at a time.

CONTENTS

PART I

THE WORLD THAT MADE THE
GENERATION ALPHA

CHAPTER 1

THE GENERATIONS THAT BUILT THE WORLD

"Each generation leaves behind both a blueprint and a question. The next must decide which to follow, and which to rewrite." - *Santiago Dagon*

Every generation inherits a world already in motion. Roads laid down earlier where people travel. Ideas formed long ago influence what feels possible now. Before we look at the New Humanity Shift, it helps to notice how the ground beneath it was prepared.

The generations that came before Generation Alpha did more than pass down customs and technologies. They shaped the emotional tone of modern life. Each generation responded to the conditions it faced, scarcity or abundance, stability or upheaval, isolation, or connection. In doing so, they left behind not only systems and institutions, but habits of attention, ways of relating, and assumptions about what it means to succeed, belong, or feel secure.

Much of the twentieth century was organized around endurance and expansion. Progress was measured by growth, productivity, and control over uncertainty. Later generations began to question the cost of that momentum. Awareness widened to include emotional health, identity, and the unseen effects of speed. These shifts did not replace what came before. They layered upon it.

The New Humanity Shift emerges from this layering. It reflects a moment when inherited systems meet new conditions. Constant connection alters how people experience time, authority, and belonging. Emotional awareness moves from the background into shared life. Leadership begins to rely less on command and more on coherence. These changes did not arrive suddenly. They have been forming across generations, often subtly, through adaptation rather than intention.

Generation Alpha enters this landscape without memory of a disconnected world. They are not starting from the same assumptions their grandparents or parents carried. Their questions arise from a different baseline. Understanding how earlier generations built the world helps explain why this New Humanity Shift feels both unfamiliar and inevitable.

This chapter looks back not to assign credit or fault, but to notice patterns. How each generation responded to its moment. How emotional priorities changed alongside material conditions. How the past continues to influence the present, even as something new begins to take shape.

What follows is a series of observations and short reflections. Notice what connects with your own experience. Consider how life may be evolving and what these changes could mean in the years ahead.

The Builders And The Dreamers

History often feels like a long current. It rises, settles, and rises again, shaped by the rhythm of every group that has carried its hopes across time. When we look for the beginning of Generation Alpha's story, we discover that it begins far behind them. It begins with those who rebuilt the world after deep hardship.

The Builders, born in the early decades of the twentieth century, grew up with scarcity close to their hands. They understood hunger. They understood duty. For them, progress was not an idea to debate. It was what allowed families to make it through one more season. A stable job, a roof that held during storms, a community that stayed together. These were victories that shaped their identity. Their trust rested in order, in shared responsibility, in structures that brought stability after so much social and political uncertainty.

The Dreamers arrived next. The Baby Boomers were born into recovery and expanding opportunity. Television flickered in family rooms. Advertising promised possibility. There was a sense that anything could change, and perhaps everything should. The Dreamers looked beyond stability toward purpose itself. They sang, marched, questioned, and pushed against limits that once felt permanent. They brought movements that reshaped culture. Their rebellion often came from a place of care rather than anger.

"The Builders taught us how to endure. The Dreamers taught us how to look beyond what survival demands."
- Santiago Dagon

Their vision reshaped society and their era carried its own tension. Growth encouraged consumption. Rising freedom encouraged restlessness. Voices that called for change also revealed hidden fractures. The Dreamers left a legacy of creativity and contradiction. Both continue to echo today.

Generation X - The Silent Bridge

Between two periods of sweeping change stood Generation X. Their entrance into history was not dramatic or loudly announced. After school, many would return to an empty home, unlock the door themselves, and spend the afternoon silently learning to be independent. The television filled the room with sound. Just as often, it was their own thoughts that kept them company.

Generation X grew familiar with self-reliance early. With working parents and fewer daily check-ins, many learned to solve problems alone, to entertain themselves, and to make sense of the world without constant guidance. That independence became both their strength and their inheritance.

They lived through the shift from analog to digital. From paper letters to early screens. They watched their world move from slower rhythms to faster ones. Many learned skepticism because they saw institutions falter. Many discovered independence not as a choice, but as a necessity. Guidance was often limited, and so they learned to rely on their own judgment. They entered adulthood without a detailed roadmap, and they adjusted to shifting expectations, new technologies, and changing cultural norms with resilience.

They valued flexibility. They preferred realism over ideals. They balanced caution with creativity. Under that independence lived solitude. It came from knowing that belonging could change without warning.

"Every bridge carries the weight of two directions. Generation X learned how to stand there without losing themselves."- *Santiago Dagon*

Their children, including many in Generation Alpha, absorbed that resilience almost by example. It was not announced or displayed loudly. It was carried in actions, in consistency, in a voice that did not need volume to convey strength.

Millennials - The Hopeful Hustlers

Millennials entered adulthood as the world finished wiring itself together. Screens became extensions of curiosity. Keyboards became early instruments of voice. They grew up with the promise that opportunity was everywhere. They came of age amid economic shocks, rising debt, unstable work, and constant comparison. Possibility and pressure arrived together.

They adapted quickly. When traditional paths narrowed, they improvised. When security felt uncertain, they diversified. Hustle became both strategy and identity. Many learned to build value through creativity, flexibility, and self-direction rather than through long term guarantees. They reshaped work, communication, and culture by necessity as much as by choice.

Beneath that momentum, deeper questions surfaced. What counts as success when effort never seems to end? Whether accumulation brings relief or simply more pressure. Whether productivity alone can satisfy the human need for purpose and balance. These questions did not halt progress. They redirected it.

"Every generation must decide what wealth truly means. The Millennials reminded us that meaning grows best in a calm heart." - *Santiago Dagon*

Through their choices, empathy reentered public conversation. Millennials helped normalize discussions around mental health, emotional awareness, and inner life. They questioned cultures of burnout and reframed ambition to include sustainability and purpose. In doing so, they revealed a tension that still shapes the present moment.

Their legacy is not just the systems they created, but the important questions they forced people to face. They showed that technology without humanity feels incomplete. They carried forward the realization that progress requires more than speed and scale. It also requires understanding what makes a life feel worth living.

Generation Z - The Awakening

If Millennials were shaped by optimism, Generation Z came of age with heightened awareness. What previous generations might have learned about days later through headlines, they witnessed live, in images and updates that made distant events feel close and immediate.

Little remained out of view. The distance between local and global collapsed. Information did not arrive slowly. It came suddenly, often labeled "Breaking News." For many people, the world no longer felt distant. It felt close and personal.

Their humor often leaned toward irony, a way of coping with a world that felt overwhelming. Beneath that tone was a deep seriousness about what they valued. Fairness matters to them. Authenticity matters. They tended to question what feels performative and support what feels real.

When it comes to friendship, physical closeness was no longer the primary foundation. Many of their relationships begin not in neighborhoods or classrooms, but in shared interests, shared challenges, and shared emotional language.

Their awareness, however, created its own strain. Constant connection sometimes became comparison. Expression sometimes became exposure. They were exposed to more information about the world than any generation before them. That constant awareness shaped Generation Z in powerful ways, even beneath the confidence they often showed.

"To notice everything is a form of strength. To remain grounded while noticing is a form of wisdom."

- Santiago Dagon

Generation Alpha is growing up with these examples in front of them. They are paying attention, even when no one thinks they are.

They take in the courage they see. They notice the honesty. They begin to understand that speaking truth does not have to mean being harsh. And they are learning that kindness is not weakness. It can be one of the strongest choices a person makes.

The Inheritance Of Momentum

Every generation leaves more than its achievements. It leaves energy that keeps moving forward. That energy is shaped by how it responded to the challenges and opportunities of its time. The Builders contributed to discipline and endurance. The Dreamers widened the horizon with vision. Generation X learned how to adapt between systems. Millennials brought empathy back into public conversation. Generation Z heightened awareness of emotional and social reality.

Generation Alpha receives all of this at once.

They are born into a world already in motion, where ideas turn into action with remarkable speed and visibility. Creation no longer waits. Expression travels instantly. Influence spreads before reflection has time to settle. In this environment, Generation Alpha may not struggle most with creating new things. Their greater challenge may be learning how to choose wisely.

The New Humanity Shift begins to take shape here. When everything asks for attention, choosing what matters becomes a defining skill. When quick reactions are praised, taking time to think becomes a sign of maturity. As systems move faster, the ability to stay grounded and steady without losing direction becomes more important than ever.

Generation Alpha inherits tools of extraordinary power, alongside emotional patterns shaped by earlier responses to change. They step into structures built for speed, scale, and reach. Their task is not to discard this inheritance, but to interpret it. To decide what to carry forward and what to question. To sense when momentum supports life and when it begins to erode it.

They will need to learn how to remain calm in environments that rarely pause. How to reflect when immediacy dominates. How to face complex issues without forcing quick or simple answers. These capacities do not replace innovation. They guide it.

"The foundation may be strong, but the spirit must be tended. Every generation builds a house. Only a few remember to let it breathe." - *Santiago Dagon*

The inheritance of momentum offers both strength and responsibility. What Generation Alpha does with it may shape not only what the world becomes, but how it feels to live within it.

Lessons From The Past, Maps For The Future

Seen in retrospect, a pattern of preparation takes shape. The Builders practiced unity through effort. The Dreamers pushed toward freedom and possibility. Generation X learned how to balance what endured with what was changing. Millennials rediscovered purpose beneath pressure. Generation Z insisted on honesty and emotional truth. Together, these movements formed a path that leads naturally to Generation Alpha.

The world Generation Alpha inherits overflows with information. It still seeks wisdom. Their opportunity may be to blend knowledge with empathy, and innovation with discernment. They are arriving at a moment that invites building not only with intelligence, but with awareness of what truly supports a meaningful human life.

"The past does not sit behind us. It rests within the choices we make now. When we act with awareness, we shape the future with care." - *Santiago Dagon*

Through much of history, the central question was survival. How to endure. How to overcome. Increasingly, a different question comes into focus. What does it mean to live well? This New Humanity Shift signals a hopeful turn. It suggests that humanity has created enough stability to begin by asking deeper questions about purpose, responsibility, and care.

Change may happen in many places at the same time. It may appear in growing emotional awareness that values understanding more than quick reaction. In ethical reflection that weighs impact alongside intention. In renewed curiosity about purpose that sits comfortably beside science and progress. These changes may appear in everyday exchanges, in how fairness is defined, and in how responsibility is shared.

In this context, progress takes on a broader meaning. Growth and speed still matter, but they are not the full measure of success. Another standard becomes just as important: depth. The ability to understand others. The choice to pause and think before acting. Empathy and awareness begin to stand alongside innovation as true signs of advancement.

As the path continues forward, the guiding question may shift again. Not how much can be built, but how thoughtfully it is built, and who it serves along the way.

"We are the ancestors of tomorrow. What we teach today will one day move within them as instinct."

- Santiago Dagon

Taken together, these lessons offer more than history. They provide orientation. They suggest that the future is not a break from what came before, but a continuation shaped by greater understanding. And in that continuity, there is room for optimism, creativity, and a deeper sense of what it means to be human.

Closing Reflection

Every generation leaves more behind than structures and systems. It leaves a tone. A rhythm. A way of responding to pressure, possibility, and change. This chapter has traced those layers not to rank them, but to understand how the present moment came to feel the way it does.

The builders shaped stability through effort and endurance. The dreamers widened the horizon. Generation X learned to move between worlds, carrying skepticism and adaptability in equal measure. Millennials brought urgency and hope into systems already straining under speed. Generation Z began questioning not only what the world does, but how it feels to live inside it. None of these movements replaced the ones before. They stacked. They interacted. They accelerated one another.

What Generation Alpha inherits is not a blank slate. It is momentum. Systems already in motion. Ideas already amplified. Tensions already present. Alongside this inheritance comes something else. A growing awareness that speed alone cannot guide what comes next.

The New Humanity Shift emerges from this realization. It does not reject the past. It integrates it. Lessons carried forward become reference points rather than rules. What worked before is examined rather than assumed. Emotional awareness, once secondary, moves closer to the center.

This chapter suggests that history is not simply behind us. It continues to operate through habits, expectations, and definitions of success that still shape daily life. Understanding those influences makes it easier to see why the present feels unsettled and why new questions are forming.

The path forward does not discard what earlier generations built. It asks how those foundations can support deeper understanding rather than constant acceleration. The future is shaped not only by innovation, but by interpretation.

As the story turns toward Generation Alpha, the emphasis changes. The attention moves from what was built to how it is lived each day. It shifts from inheritance to intention. The next chapters consider what happens when a new generation grows up inside the world created by those before them and begins to decide what kind of humanity it wants to carry forward.

CHAPTER 2

THE GREAT ACCELERATION

"The future did not arrive as a visitor. It grew inside the way we live." - *Santiago Dagon*

Change has always been part of human life, but its pace has not always felt this intense. Over the past few decades, time itself seems to have compressed. Information moves faster than reflection. Decisions are made before their consequences fully appear. The distance between action and response has narrowed to the point where life often feels immediate rather than unfolding.

This period can be described as a Great Acceleration. It is not caused by one invention or single event, but by many forces working at the same time. Digital connection, global trade, economic demands, cultural exposure, and environmental pressure all move together. The result is a world that seldom slows down on its own.

The New Humanity Shift begins within this acceleration, not outside it. Rather than resisting speed alone, people begin to notice how speed shapes attention, emotion, and judgment.

What changes is not only how fast life moves, but how deeply it is felt. Emotional experience becomes denser. Awareness is tested by volume rather than scarcity.

Generation Alpha grows up inside this tempo. They do not remember a slower baseline. Instant access, constant feedback, and overlapping realities form the conditions of their early lives. Because of this, they often adapt in ways that look different from earlier generations. They sense overload quickly. They recognize inconsistency early. They respond less to authority that rushes and more to guidance that helps them interpret what they are experiencing.

Acceleration alters leadership as well. Influence shifts away from speed alone and toward the ability to remain clear when everything moves quickly. The capacity to pause, notice, and choose gains importance in environments where reaction is easy and reflection feels rare. As life speeds up, awareness becomes more important, not less.

This chapter explores how speed reshapes emotional life. How constant connection influences regulation, empathy, and attention. How children growing up in accelerated conditions may develop different expectations of learning, leadership, and relationships. These changes are not uniform or simple. They appear uneven, layered, and still forming.

As you read, reflect on where these ideas feel familiar in your own life. Observe how similar patterns may be unfolding in the children you see each day. This is not about forecasting outcomes, but about understanding how emotional development may be evolving and why that evolution matters for the future.

A World That Outruns Itself

Every age believes it is moving faster than the one before it. For Generation Alpha, this feeling is no illusion. The world truly has begun to outrun itself.

A century ago, discovery unfolded slowly. A new idea would appear, settle over years, and gradually shape the habits of its time. Now the distance between invention and adoption has collapsed. Updates arrive overnight. A tool introduced this morning may be replaced before evening. Generation Alpha is growing up surrounded by systems that adjust on their own, machines that adapt, and networks that remain constantly awake.

Progress has become so continuous that many barely notice it. It fades into the background, like a vibration mistaken for stillness. An Alpha child may never experience a world without this constant movement. Connection will feel as ordinary as air, familiar and necessary.

"We built machines to save time, and then we filled the saved time with more machines." - *Santiago Dagon*

The challenge ahead may not revolve around creating faster tools. It may center on developing stronger inner grounding. As systems accelerate, human character becomes more important, not less.

The question may not be how quickly we can move, but whether we can move forward without losing clarity about who we are and what matters. In times of rapid change, remembering our values may shape the direction more than any new device ever could.

The Physics Of Modern Life

Acceleration is not only about machines or technology. It is emotional as well. Human awareness once developed around the slower rhythms of nature: the rising sun, the changing seasons, the steady work of the soil. Today, that slower way of life has been replaced by nonstop activity that almost never stops. A question forms, and the answer appears before curiosity can even stretch. A desire flickers, and an algorithm predicts it instantly. The small gap between wanting and receiving has nearly vanished. Imagination, once fueled by waiting, now has very little room to roam.

Generation Alpha raised in this environment will adapt with remarkable skill. They may think in networks rather than lines. They may absorb information in flashes rather than steps. They may improvise more naturally than any generation before them. This speed may also steal the patience that gives understanding its depth. When everything moves quickly, silence can feel uncomfortable.

"When speed becomes the norm, stillness becomes a revolution."- *Santiago Dagon*

Stillness may become a new form of evolution. It protects awareness in a world that rarely stops.

The End Of Waiting

There was a time when waiting felt purposeful. Letters took days to arrive. Harvests took months to grow. Relationships deepened over years. These intervals taught people how to trust what had not yet appeared.

Today, waiting is often viewed as a problem to solve. A short delay can cause irritation. A message that takes longer than expected can feel disruptive. In a culture built on instant access, speed easily becomes associated with competence and success.

Earlier generations experienced more friction in everyday life. Information took time. Responses required patience. That delay was not always pleasant, but it created space for anticipation. It also shaped appreciation. When something required effort or time, it often carried greater meaning.

As immediacy becomes standard, it is worth noticing what disappears with it. The pause once offered perspective. It allowed people to reflect, to value what arrived, and to recognize the human effort behind it.

The space between desire and fulfillment once allowed wonder to take shape. Something was gained simply through anticipation.

"Without the space between beats, there can be no rhythm."
- Santiago Dagon

For Generation Alpha, patience may become an unfamiliar skill in a world built around immediacy. When everything responds instantly, the value of waiting is not always obvious.

However, something develops in that space. Reflection. A deeper engagement with what eventually arrives. Understanding does not always appear at the moment of access. It often takes shape in the time that leads up to it.

If this generation comes to experience that rhythm, they may rediscover a sense of wonder that cannot be downloaded or accelerated. Some insights require time. And time, when allowed to do its work, changes how things are understood.

Information Without Absorption

Humanity now generates more data in a single week than entire civilizations once produced over centuries. Yet information alone does not create understanding.

Information is no longer scarce. It arrives continuously, in headlines, feeds, videos, and alerts. What is less common is time to process it. Many people gather more than they examine. Minds stay full, while deeper understanding can feel stretched thin.

Generation Alpha will grow up surrounded by uninterrupted streams of content. Access will not be their challenge. Interpretation may be. When everything is easy to access, the important skill changes. It is not about learning more facts. It is about knowing which facts are truly worth your time and attention.

As they grow older, Generation Alpha may need to learn the difference between information that helps them grow and information that drains their energy. They will need to tell apart what teaches them something useful from what simply distracts them. In a world full of constant input, the ability to choose wisely may become one of the most important kinds of intelligence.

"Wisdom is not the sum of what we know, but what we choose to remember." - *Santiago Dagon*

Their devices will answer any question. But only a human soul can form the questions that truly matter.

The Myth Of Efficiency

Modern life often treats speed and efficiency as signs of progress. Systems promise to make things easier. Tools remove effort and save time. Each upgrade seems to simplify life, but it can also create a new kind of pressure. When everything is optimized, life can start to feel rushed instead of meaningful.

Ease is often confused with real satisfaction. When every step is guided and obstacles are quietly removed, discovery becomes less exciting. Without wrong turns or uncertainty, learning feels predictable. When there is no space to wander, there is less chance to find something surprising or new.

Children growing up in the Alpha era often move through carefully planned schedules. Free moments do not always appear naturally in that structure. Unplanned time can become rare. Time without clear goals, instructions, or deadlines sometimes stands apart from the rest. In those open spaces, curiosity tends to lead rather than outcomes.

"Perfection is sterile. Only the unfinished can grow."
- Santiago Dagon

In this setting, what looks like inefficiency can start to mean something different. It can become a space where exploration happens without pressure. Wandering gives attention room to expand. From that space, curiosity grows. And curiosity remains central to creativity, learning, and human development.

Acceleration And Anxiety

As the pace of life increases, the human nervous system can feel the strain. Constant alerts, shifting news cycles, and uninterrupted connection place pressure on attention and emotion. Anxiety often rises alongside acceleration.

In a culture shaped by visibility, recognition is frequently linked to how often one is seen or acknowledged. Metrics become signals of worth. When comparison begins to replace self-understanding, something internal can shift. A lingering discomfort appears, not always dramatic, but persistent.

For Generation Alpha, growing up within this environment may influence how identity forms. The tension between visibility and authenticity is not abstract. It plays out daily, in small interactions and ongoing evaluations of self.

Generation Alpha will inherit systems that constantly reflect them back to themselves. Notifications, reactions, comments, metrics. Each one offering feedback. Each one hinting at who they are, or who they are expected to become. These digital mirrors operate without pause.

As Santiago Dagon writes, "**A mirror that never sleeps will one day forget what it reflects**."

When reflection is continuous, clarity can blur. Identity risks being shaped by response rather than formed through understanding.

In this environment, the inner self becomes increasingly important. Not as a catch phrase, but as a practical need. Generation Alpha children may benefit from experiences that help them define themselves beyond screens, beyond approval cycles, beyond public evaluation. The capacity to return to one's own thinking, one's own values, may influence how confidently they move through a world that is always watching.

The Acceleration Of Empathy

Even within this speed, there is unexpected grace. The same networks that scatter attention can also carry compassion. Awareness of suffering travels faster now. So does the call for help.

Generation Alpha is growing up with a broader view of humanity than most generations before them. A child can now witness events across the globe in real time and speak with peers thousands of miles away as easily as with someone next door. That exposure may shape how they understand belonging. Strangers can feel familiar. Distant communities can feel relevant.

As Santiago Dagon writes, "**When hearts connect as fast as signals, a new form of healing begins**."

This expanded awareness brings possibility, but also complexity. When suffering is visible everywhere, emotional intensity can accumulate. The challenge may not be a lack of feeling. It may be learning how to carry those feelings without becoming consumed by them.

Empathy, when grounded, can guide thoughtful action. Without direction, it can overwhelm. How this generation learns to balance awareness with resilience may influence how compassion takes shape in the years ahead.

Living In The Age Of Now

The present moment no longer occupies a single place. Life unfolds in physical settings while attention also moves through digital networks. For Generation Alpha, shifting between these layers often feels natural. The boundaries that once separated online and offline experience appear thinner, more permeable.

In this environment, it becomes easier to live everywhere at once. Screens invite constant engagement. Motion fills empty spaces. Stimulation replaces pause. Engagement itself does not require withdrawal from the moment. It depends on how attention is carried through it.

"Awareness is not the absence of movement. It is the attention that moves with it." - *Santiago Dagon*

For children growing up inside this rhythm, the challenge is not technology alone. It is learning how to remain connected to what is directly in front of them while navigating wider worlds at the same time. When digital experience expands perception without narrowing relationships, the present moment does not disappear. It becomes layered, holding both connection and closeness at once.

The Paradox Of Progress

Progress has rarely come without tradeoffs. Every improvement brings some kind of change. Connection expands, and silence becomes harder to find. Access increases, and depth can be harder to sustain. Abundance grows, and simplicity can feel distant.

The period often described as The Great Acceleration has intensified this pattern. Systems move faster. Decisions ripple outward more quickly. Output increases. But speed alone does not create purpose. When movement becomes the primary measure, clarity can thin. Activity can replace intentions.

As Santiago Dagon writes, **"The world does not need to move faster. It needs to move with purpose."**

Generation Alpha is growing up in a fast-moving world. Their comfort with technology is not the main issue. What matters more is how they choose to use it. Tools can encourage constant consumption, or they can help people care for one another. Systems can increase pressure, or they can reflect shared values.

The choices this generation makes will not erase complexity. But they may influence direction. Growth, in their hands, could become less about expansion for its own sake and more about alignment between innovation and human priorities.

Learning To Breathe Again

Each era must relearn what it has forgotten. For Generation Alpha the forgotten art may be the simple act of breathing without hurry.

To breathe consciously is to reclaim time. It is a reminder that awareness is not a luxury. It is a foundation. If Generation Alpha children learn how to rest inside their own attention, then acceleration becomes less of a threat. It becomes a teacher.

"Speed becomes harmful only when it outruns awareness. Awareness turns motion into evolution." - *Santiago Dagon*

The Great Acceleration does not have to be understood as a competition. It is better described as a pattern in motion, a shift in tempo across technology, culture, and daily life. When everything speeds up, it can feel like a race. But speed itself is not the goal. It is simply part of the times we live in.

Seen this way, the task is not to resist movement or to fear it. It is to understand it. To notice where it leads. To decide how to respond within it. It requires clarity about direction. The future will continue to unfold. The question is how Generation Alpha chooses to move within it, and what intentions shape that movement.

Closing Reflection

The Great Acceleration does not simply change how fast the world moves. It changes how life is felt. Time stretches and compresses. Distance loses significance. Attention is pulled in many directions at once. For children growing up inside these conditions, speed is not an event. It is the atmosphere.

Across this chapter, a pattern begins to surface. Acceleration amplifies everything. Opportunity expands. Risk sharpens. Learning quickens. So does exhaustion. The nervous system absorbs these forces long before the mind learns how to name them. What looks like adaptation on the surface often carries hidden effort underneath.

Generation Alpha is not encountering acceleration as a disruption to an earlier rhythm. It is their starting point. Because of this, their needs are not centered on speed itself, but on interpretation. How to make sense of constant input. How to recover after intensity. How to tell the difference between urgency and importance.

For adults, acceleration brings a different responsibility. Not to slow the world, which may not be possible, but to help children recognize when speed begins to erode clarity. To notice when attention fractures. To model how reflection can exist alongside momentum.

The New Humanity Shift suggests that resilience does not come from keeping pace. It grows through judgment. Through knowing when to engage and when to step back. Through understanding that adaptation is not only about endurance, but about purpose.

Speed will likely keep increasing. What can change is how people handle it. When awareness grows along with speed, it becomes less overwhelming. It turns into something people can manage and move through with intention.

The question this chapter leaves open is not how fast the future will move, but how thoughtfully humanity learns to move within it.

CHAPTER 3

THE DIGITAL WOMB

**"Before they open their eyes, they are already seen.
Before they speak, they are already heard."**
- Santiago Dagon

Every generation is shaped by its earliest environment. For Generation Alpha, that environment includes a digital layer present from the beginning of life. Screens, signals, and networks surround their first experiences, often before language forms and long before memory settles. Connection is not introduced later. It is already there.

This chapter uses the phrase Digital Womb to describe that condition. Not as judgment, and not as alarm, but as observation. Just as earlier generations were shaped by neighborhoods, households, or broadcast media, Generation Alpha is shaped by a world where information flows continuously and boundaries between physical and digital experience are thin.

The New Humanity Shift takes shape inside this environment. Constant connection changes how children perceive closeness, separation, and belonging. Attention is shaped early by responsiveness. Emotion is influenced by feedback loops that arrive without delay. These conditions do not determine outcomes, but they alter the starting point from which development unfolds.

For Generation Alpha, the digital world does not feel artificial. It feels ambient. It hums in the background of daily life, influencing how curiosity forms, how reassurance is sought, and how identity begins to organize. This does not replace human relationships, but it reshapes how relationship is experienced, mediated, and understood.

Leadership and concern adapt in response. Adults find themselves guiding children not only through physical spaces, but through invisible ones. Emotional development increasingly depends on interpretation, helping children make sense of constant input rather than shielding them from it entirely. The New Humanity Shift suggests that awareness becomes more important as exposure increases.

This chapter explores what it means to begin life within continuous connection. How early digital immersion interacts with attachment, attention, and emotional regulation. How children raised in this environment may relate differently to authority, trust, and meaning. These patterns remain fluid. They are not fixed traits, but responses to conditions still evolving.

As repeated before, read these sections as reflections rather than declarations. The goal is not to predict the future, but to understand how life may be changing and what those changes might lead to.

The First Cradle Of Connection

Every generation begins inside a particular atmosphere. The Builders were shaped by industry and struggle. The Dreamers were shaped by television and cultural awakening. Generation Alpha begins life wrapped in the mellow glow of screens, a cradle that stays awake before dawn and long after sleep.

Even before birth, their lives move through networks. Images appear in ultrasound posts. Names echo in family chats. The first breath becomes a notification. The first laughter becomes a small video that circles across continents. Moments that once belonged only to family now drift into the wider world with a single tap.

We often call it sharing, but it also involves release. The memories we preserve may feel personal and meaningful, especially for those they are meant for. At the same time, once shared, they become visible to many others. They are held in systems and spaces designed to remember, even when we might later wish they could fade.

"The first act of modern love is to announce it. But the truest love still happens, where the world cannot see."

- Santiago Dagon

This digital world surrounds many Generation Alpha children even before they are born. It records moments. It influences what they see and how others see them. Within this constant flow of connection, a child may begin life already linked to people and places beyond their own home, long before they understand where they belong.

The Home That Never Powers Down

Most homes now breathe with invisible circuits. Voices answer from corners when summoned. Music floats into the air without request. Screens shift their glow to match our moods. These conveniences ease daily strain. They soothe restless children. They fill long evenings. In offering such ease, they also thin the edges that once defined what it meant to offer genuine human connection.

A parent once sang into darkness, never sure if the melody would soothe. Now an artificial voice perfectly sings each time. The comfort remains, but the exchange of human connections grows fainter.

"Answers without journey starve the soul of meaning."
- Santiago Dagon

The line between attention and automation grows more delicate each year. A Generation Alpha child may receive quick responses, but there may not always be a real person behind them. The task of modern parenting may not be removing technology but humanizing it. It means teaching that love is not measured by how quickly something responds, but by the deeper attentiveness that waits to listen.

When The Screen Becomes A Mirror

For a child growing up now, a screen does not feel distant or mechanical. It responds. A finger touches the surface, and something moves. A sound triggers animation. A question produces an answer. Cause and effect appear immediately, almost seamless. It can give the impression that the world itself is responding to desire.

But what is reflected back is only a simulation. It can mirror emotion without experiencing it. It can display affection without understanding it. The digital face smiles on cue, unchanged by context. It does not fatigue. It does not struggle with doubt. It does not wrestle with conflicting feelings.

That distinction matters. The interaction feels responsive, but it does not carry the complexity of a human exchange. Understanding that difference may shape how Generation Alpha defines relationship, expectation, and trust in the years ahead.

"A mirror that always smiles will never teach us who we are." *-Santiago Dagon*

In this environment, adults often find themselves acting as interpreters. They help children distinguish between automated response and human relationship. A device reacts. A person listens. A system answers. A human offers understanding.

That difference is not always obvious at first to the Generation Alpha child. It has to be experienced. Repeatedly. Through misunderstandings that require explanation. Through moments when someone pauses to consider another's feeling.

Real human connection includes awkwardness, patience, and tuning. It includes effort. And in that effort, something forms that no programmed reaction can replicate. Over time, those lived exchanges teach the Generation Alpha child what authenticity feels like.

The Vanishing Boundary

Childhood was once shaped by familiar places. The yard. The street. The nearby woods. The safe distance from home to school. Now the map has no edges. A Generation Alpha child may explore the planet before learning to tie shoes.

This expansion is extraordinary. Young minds encounter the full spectrum of human experience too early. Joy and cruelty. Wonder and confusion. The world arrives all at once.

"Freedom without guidance is a compass without north."
- Santiago Dagon

We cannot return to the kind of sheltered childhood that once existed. But we can help children develop healthy limits based on awareness instead of strict control. Safety now grows from the ability to pause, think, and ask questions before reacting. For Generation Alpha, home may become less about a physical space and more about a sense of balance they carry within themselves wherever they are.

Memory Without Forgetting

In earlier times, memory faded slowly. Photographs yellowed in sharpest. Stories drifted from detail to essence. Mistakes lost their sharp edges and became lessons. Now nearly nothing disappears. Every image, every sentence, every impulsive moment lingers somewhere in vast archives that are rarely forgotten.

This permanence reshapes identity. The mercy of forgetting becomes harder to find. Generation Alpha children may grow up under the pressure of their own digital history, learning to see themselves not only through present growth but through preserved versions of past selves.

"When nothing can be erased, forgiveness becomes sacred."
-Santiago Dagon

Parents document childhood out of care. Photos, videos, saved messages. Each one captures a stage that feels important in the moment. Technology makes preservation easy, and the intention behind it is often love.

At the same time, constant recording can shape how growth unfolds. When every phase is stored and replayed, it can be harder to leave earlier versions behind. Development requires movement. It requires freedom to change without being permanently defined by a past moment.

In a culture that records almost everything, learning how to let go may become more important. This does not mean hiding the truth but allowing room for growth and change. Generation Alpha children benefit from honesty. They also benefit from the freedom to mature beyond earlier versions of themselves without those moments being replayed forever.

The Mindful Parent

Raising a Generation Alpha child in a connected world requires awareness and trust at the same time. Parents are learning to notice what is happening beyond the surface. To hear what is being expressed beneath distraction. To recognize when

Generation Alpha engagement with a screen is about curiosity, escape, boredom, or belonging.

There will be evenings when a device captures a child's focus more quickly than a parent's request. That reality does not signal failure. It reflects the environment children are growing up in. What becomes important is how reconnection happens.

When a parent circles back after tension or misunderstanding, something meaningful is modeled. Repair becomes visible. Persistence becomes visible. The message communicated is not control, but commitment. Over time, that pattern teaches resilience more effectively than enforcement alone.

"The child does not need a perfect parent. They need a parent who can return." - *Santiago Dagon*

Shared curiosity can become a bridge between generations. Sitting side by side. Watching something together. Asking questions without rushing to correct. Thinking out loud about what something means. These small acts build understanding.

When a parent engages in this way, conversation deepens. Language grows more expressive. A Generation Alpha child learns not only facts, but how to explore ideas with another person. That is where emotional fluency begins.

In a world filled with advanced systems and intelligent tools, human engagement still shapes development in ways no device can replicate. The most influential technology in a child's life may still be a caring adult willing to pay attention.

The Soul Of Solitude

In a culture filled with constant signals, uninterrupted time alone has become less common. Notifications arrive. Background audio continues. Screens remain within reach. Solitude can feel unfamiliar, even uncomfortable.

Many developmental psychologists have long noted the importance of unstructured internal time. Imagination often forms when external input slows. Reflection develops when thought is not immediately interrupted. Without space for internal dialogue, creativity and emotional depth can narrow.

The connected environment surrounding Generation Alpha children is immersive. Sound and motion rarely stop. A child may move from one stream of input to another without extended stillness. In that rhythm, hearing one's own thinking can become more difficult.

Solitude, however, is not isolation. It is an encounter with one's internal landscape. As Santiago Dagon writes, "In silence, the self remembers its original language."

Creating room for that experience may require intention. Devices can be set aside, not as a disciplinary act, but as an opening. When Generation Alpha children are given time without immediate stimulation, discomfort may appear first. If allowed to continue, something else often follows: imagination, reflection, and new ideas. In those gaps, the inner world becomes visible again, and with it, a deeper understanding of self.

The Awakening Within The Network

Even within its noise, the digital realm carries possibility. Every shared glance, every question, every small reflection a Generation Alpha child sees on a screen becomes part of an inner search. When the child sees their own face shining back at them, they begin a lifelong inquiry: Who am I in this expanding world?

If encouraged with awareness, this question becomes profound. Generation Alpha children may grow into a generation that blends emotion with science. They may sense empathy even through distance. They may build bridges between code and compassion in ways that are still beyond our imagination.

"The world that surrounds them has changed, but the ancient call within them remains the same."
- Santiago Dagon

The Digital Womb is not a cage. It is a chrysalis. Within its glow, a new form of human development begins.

Closing Reflection

Generation Alpha arrives in a world already in dialogue with them. Data is gathered early. Systems respond before a sentence is fully formed. Information surrounds daily life in ways that feel seamless and immediate.

The core of a child remains unchanged. Curiosity. The search for belonging. The desire to understand where one fits within something larger. Those impulses are not new. They are part of the human story across generations.

The task before adults is not separation from technology. It is interpretation. Generation Alpha children will benefit from learning how to engage tools with awareness rather than allowing those tools to define identity. Technology can reflect interest, creativity, even connection. It does not determine value.

As Santiago Dagon writes, "**The Digital Womb surrounds them, but the human heart must still raise them**."

When that distinction remains clear, technological systems become part of the environment rather than the authority within it. Devices can support communication and learning without replacing human influence. In that balance, innovation and care move together, and the human voice continues to shape the transformation of society and culture.

PART II

THE INNER ARCHITECTURE

CHAPTER 4

CURIOSITY UNBOUND

"Curiosity is the first language of the soul. It asks questions long before words exist." - *Santiago Dagon*

Curiosity has always driven learning. But now the conditions surrounding it have changed. For earlier generations, curiosity often moved slowly. Questions led to libraries, conversations, or careful trial and error. For Generation Alpha, curiosity unfolds in a world where answers appear almost instantly, and exploration happens across many channels at once.

This chapter explores what curiosity looks like when limits dissolve. Information is no longer scarce. It is abundant, searchable, and constantly updating. The New Humanity Shift takes shape within this abundance, altering how children ask questions, follow interests, and make sense of what they find.

For Generation Alpha, curiosity is rarely confined to a single subject or pathway. Interests branch quickly. Learning crosses boundaries between disciplines, platforms, and experiences. This freedom expands possibilities. It also introduces new challenges. Knowing where to look becomes less difficult than knowing what to hold onto.

Curiosity unbound changes emotional development as well. Wonder can deepen Generation Alpha engagement, but constant access can also fragment attention. Children learn early how to navigate overload, discern relevance, and balance exploration with rest. These skills become part of emotional intelligence rather than academic technique.

Mentorship within this New Humanity Shift responds differently to curiosity. Guidance moves away from controlling information and toward helping children interpret it. The role of adults becomes less about supplying answers and more about helping young minds develop judgment, patience, and trust in their own questions.

This chapter examines how curiosity functions within constant connection. How imagination, attention, and emotional regulation interact when exploration has few external limits. How Generation Alpha may redefine learning as participation rather than accumulation. These patterns remain open and evolving, shaped by context as much as by temperament.

What follows does not present final answers. It offers a collection of reflections and short examinations. Each theme highlights ways emotional development may evolve within a culture defined by ongoing connection and rapid change. The purpose is not to forecast outcomes, but to consider how the life we have known may be transforming.

The Birth Of Infinite Learning

Every Generation Alpha child begins as an explorer. Hands reach out. Eyes study movement and texture. The world becomes a laboratory of sensation and experiment. Curiosity has always been one of humanity's earliest tools.

For much of history, access to knowledge moved through narrow channels. Books were limited by location. Experts were separated by distance and status. Learning often depended on permission, timing, and proximity.

Today the landscape looks different. A Generation Alpha child can ask a question aloud and receive information drawn from across the globe. They can observe coral reefs from the living room. They can hear another language before breakfast. They can experiment with coding before mastering basic arithmetic. The school bell no longer involves learning within fixed hours. Knowledge flows continuously, often following interest rather than schedule.

As Santiago Dagon writes, "**The mind once asked where it could learn. Now it asks how deeply it is willing to know.**"

Expanded access brings opportunity. It also introduces complexity. Curiosity can open doors, but it can also flood attention. The challenge for adults mentoring the Generation Alpha child is not limiting inquiry but helping it find direction. When curiosity is supported with structure and reflection, it strengthens rather than overwhelms.

The following sections offer a view into the possible future of Generation Alpha within a world shaped by unlimited access to learning. What follows is not a forecast, but an examination of emerging trends. It considers how infinite access to information may shift as opportunity expands and education moves beyond traditional boundaries and how this might influence curiosity, collaboration, identity, and purpose in the years ahead.

From Answers To Awareness

Information now surrounds daily life. Questions can be spoken and answered within seconds. The speed can be reassuring. It reduces uncertainty quickly. But immediate answers do not always lead to deeper understanding.

Insight develops when the mind stays with an idea longer than the first response. Earlier generations described that process as contemplation. Today, it often requires intention. Distraction is easier than reflection.

In this environment, the role of adults has shifted. Parents and teachers are no longer the primary holders of information. Generation Alpha children can access facts independently. What becomes more important is interpretation. Adults help translate data into context. They help children examine not only what is said, but what it means.

As Santiago Dagon writes, **"To answer quickly is to end learning. To wonder longer is to begin understanding."**

The greater risk for Generation Alpha may not be a lack of knowledge. It may be the illusion of mastery that forms from surface familiarity. Exposure can feel like expertise. True learning requires time, revision, and humility.

Education, then, becomes less about immediate correctness and more about depth. There is value in not knowing. There is growth in staying with a question long enough for it to reshape the one asking it.

The Playground Of Infinite Learning

The Generation Alpha classroom may no longer be confined to a single building or a single location. Learning may begin in a shared studio space, continue in a virtual lab, and finish at a desk in a bedroom. Generation Alpha students have the ability to work across time zones as a matter of routine. A teenager in Nairobi can design a robot alongside a peer in Seoul. A child in Lisbon can exchange ideas with a farmer in Kansas and influence how a problem is understood.

As access expands, traditional hierarchies will begin to shift. Effective mentors will guide inquiry rather than dominate it. The distance between expert and learner will narrow in the years ahead.

Looking ahead at Generation Alpha, the line between play and study may continue to blur. Learning might feel less like a separate task and more like an extension of curiosity. This generation could help shape new systems of thinking and collaboration that move fluidly between imagination and structure. Short videos already show how skills can be demonstrated and absorbed in real time. Digital companions offer steady responsiveness and availability that busy human schedules do not always provide.

A different form of intelligence may take shape. It combines imagination with social awareness. It pairs experimentation with reflection. Knowledge no longer builds upward in a single line. It spreads outward, interconnected, more like a forest than a tower.

"The wise do not stand at the front of the room. They move with the questions and listen for the next one."
- Santiago Dagon

From Student To Creator

The most important New Humanity Shift is not in how Generation Alpha children learn, but in what they do with what they learn. Education once shaped listeners. Now it shapes makers.

A child writes a song before adolescence. They sketch a world before dinner. They share a thought and watch it travel further than they can imagine. Culture no longer arrives from a distant stage. It is built in real time by young hands. This creative freedom is powerful. Without grounding, however, it can dissolve into noise.

"Creation is sacred when it rises from wonder, not from the hunger to be seen." *- Santiago Dagon*

As Generation Alpha gains access to powerful tools and expanding knowledge, humility becomes an essential balance that must be intentionally taught. Skills can develop rapidly. Character usually takes longer. When ability accelerates, perspective needs the same careful attention so it can mature alongside it.

Mentors of Generation Alpha children must teach that attention shapes quality. Patience shapes understanding. Work that connects to something beyond personal recognition tends to endure. When effort serves a wider purpose, it is in depth. In that context, a child's growth is not only about achievement. It becomes part of contribution.

Companions Of Code

Digital learning companions are likely to become familiar figures in a Generation Alpha child's development. These systems can detect patterns in performance, adjust difficulty, and offer alternate explanations when frustration appears. Support is no longer limited to a single classroom or one instructor at a desk. It now exists within a network of human mentors and responsive technologies.

This New Humanity Shift expands access. It increases personalization. It can make learning more adaptive and immediate.

At the same time, there are limits to what automation provides. Precision can be programmed. Feedback can be optimized. But purpose does not originate in code. Purpose forms through lived examples, through observing how adults make choices, handle setbacks, and align effort with values.

As Santiago Dagon writes, "**A good teacher points to the stars. A wise teacher reminds the student that they are made of the same fire**."

Generation Alpha mentors must teach that tools can expand opportunity, but people give it direction. When both work together, progress becomes more than efficiency. It becomes development grounded in understanding.

Curiosity As The New Literacy

Literacy once meant the ability to read and write. Today it means the ability to notice and to question. The Generation Alpha future belongs to those who can connect ideas, sense their kinship across cultures, and follow the thread of insight even when the path turns.

"The curious do not resist the tide of change. They learn to dance with it." - *Santiago Dagon*

Generation Alpha mentors must show that curiosity can become frayed when choices become too many. True curiosity is patience. It listens for the real questions hidden beneath the noise.

The Return Of Wonder

Wonder is the frontier where science meets soul. It is the reason a child looks at the night sky and whispers why. Modern life risks dulling that whisper beneath convenience and endless stimulation.

Generation Alpha will grow up able to simulate almost anything. Simulations serve a purpose, but they cannot replace the tranquil awe that comes from real experience.

"The world does not need more information. It needs more eyes that can still widen." - *Santiago Dagon*

Adults can help sustain wonder when they allow themselves to experience it openly. When a parent pauses to marvel at something simple, without self-consciousness, a Generation Alpha child learns that curiosity does not expire with age.

Awe is not a phase to outgrow. It reflects attentiveness. It reflects the ability to notice. When adults model that kind of awareness, they show that wonder is not naïve. It is an early form of wisdom, one that continues to deepen over time.

The Discipline Of Depth

Novelty arrives without effort. Depth does not. Exposure can introduce ideas, but it does not develop understanding on its own. For Generation Alpha, learning often begins quickly. What determines growth is whether attention stays long enough to reach what lies beneath the surface.

Depth forms through return. Revisiting a question. Sitting with uncertainty. Allowing effort to extend beyond the first spark of interest. This process often includes friction. It can feel repetitive. It can feel slow. It is within this sustained engagement that understanding takes shape.

"Depth is not discovered. It is cultivated." - *Santiago Dagon*

Attention shapes identity. When children stay with a challenge long enough to work through it, they begin to see what they are capable of. Curiosity starts the process. Commitment keeps it moving, turning interest into real understanding and effort into confidence.

The Mentor's New Role

In a world where information arrives from every direction, mentors take on a different kind of importance. Their role is no longer about controlling access to knowledge. It centers on helping young people navigate abundance. They do not compete for attention. They help bring it into focus.

A mentor offers perspective shaped by lived experience. Through conversation, examples, and consistency, they reveal how knowledge connects to values, limits, and daily life. What they model often teaches more than what they explain.

"The truest mentor does not say follow me. They whisper remember who you are." - *Santiago Dagon*

When guidance takes this form, learning extends beyond skill or performance. It becomes a process of formation. Generation Alpha learners often begin by mirroring what they see, as all learners do. Over time, that imitation gives way to discernment, and a clearer sense of self begins to take shape.

The Future Classroom

Tomorrow's classroom may not always resemble rows of desks and a fixed schedule. It might unfold in a meadow, a studio, a circle of friends working through an idea, or a room where attention turns inward and breathing becomes part of learning. A Generation Alpha child could study marine ecosystems while standing beside a local river. They might explore empathy through collaborative art. Time spent in reflection may be recognized as development rather than discipline.

In that context, school becomes less about location and more about experience. It is any setting where awareness expands and understanding deepens.

As Santiago Dagon writes, **"One day the word school will mean simply wherever awakening happens."**

When learning broadens in this way, the central question begins to change. Instead of asking only, "What do I know?" students may also ask, "Who am I becoming through what I learn?" Education then returns to a deeper purpose. Knowledge becomes connected to character. Achievement becomes linked to contribution. Learning is not a race upward, but a way of finding one's place within a shared world.

Closing Reflection

Curiosity often marks the beginning of awareness. It appears early in childhood, in questions that seem endless. It also lingers late in life for those who continue to look closely at the world. When it is encouraged, curiosity can widen into empathy. It allows a person to step beyond the self and consider other lives and perspectives. When it is dismissed or rushed, it can narrow and lose its openness.

Generation Alpha inherits a planet that is more connected and more visible than at any other time. Earth becomes an accessible library, with cultures, ecosystems, and ideas available for exploration.

Their questions may lead to new tools and discoveries. They may also lead to deeper understanding of one another. Innovation and insight do not need to compete. They can develop together.

As Santiago Dagon writes, "**Curiosity is not the hunger for answers. It is the love of being alive.**"

If that orientation remains central, the next stage of human development may be guided less by speed and more by thoughtful judgment. Progress will not be defined only by what can be created, but by what truly deserves to be created.

CHAPTER 5

THE SOCIAL SHIFT

"The first lesson of friendship is not how to speak. It is how to see." – *Santiago Dagon*

Social life has always reflected the tools and conditions of its time. What changes now is the speed, scale, and visibility of connection. Conversations no longer remain local. Identity is shaped in public view. Belonging is negotiated across networks that stretch far beyond family, neighborhood, or classroom.

This chapter explores the social shift unfolding alongside the New Humanity Shift. Connection becomes continuous rather than occasional. Relationships form and dissolve with greater visibility. Emotional signals travel faster, and social feedback arrives with little delay. These conditions reshape how children learn trust, cooperation, and self-understanding.

Generation Alpha grows up within this expanded social field. They are exposed early to many voices, viewpoints, and expectations at once. Wide exposure can expand a child's perspective, but it also places greater demands on emotional regulation. Learning how to handle inclusion, comparison, and the desire to belong becomes an early and central part of development rather than something faced later in life.

Social influence changes as well. Authority is less likely to flow from position alone and more likely to emerge through authenticity and consistency. Children notice quickly when behavior and values diverge. Leadership within this social shift depends on coherence rather than control, on the ability to participate without dominating.

The New Humanity Shift reframes community itself. Connection is no longer limited by proximity. Shared experience forms across distance. At the same time, the need for meaningful relationships remains unchanged. The tension between visibility and intimacy becomes a defining feature of modern social life.

This chapter examines how social development unfolds within constant connection. How empathy, boundaries, and self-concept are shaped when interaction rarely pauses. How Generation Alpha may approach friendship, conflict, and cooperation differently from those who grew up offline. These patterns are not fixed. They continue to evolve as conditions change.

Approach these sections as thoughtful observations, not fixed conclusions. Pay attention to what resonates with your own experience. Look at the children in your life and see where these patterns may already be unfolding. The purpose is not to forecast the future, but to explore how emotional life might be changing and what those changes could suggest for the years ahead.

The New Village

For most of history, belonging grew from physical closeness. People gathered around shared spaces. Meals were passed by hand. Stories were told within circles small enough to see every face. The village was limited in size, but it carried depth.

That circle has expanded. Generation Alpha is growing up in a world where friendship often begins through a screen rather than a doorway. Companions may live across continents.

This new form of community brings both connection and complexity. A reserved child might feel understood by someone far away and still struggle to feel noticed at home. Attention divides across multiple spaces. Care can become fragmented, offered in brief exchanges rather than sustained engagement.

As Santiago Dagon writes, **"Connection without compassion is a crowd. Compassion without connection is a prayer."**

The social shift now underway calls for a different kind of awareness. Distance is no longer measured only in geography. It is measured in depth of understanding. Nearness becomes less about miles and more about genuine engagement.

The following sections explore how this evolving social environment may shape Generation Alpha. They examine emerging patterns and consider how community, identity, and belonging might develop.

The Language Of Emotion Online

Every generation invents a new way to express what sits in the heart. The Builders wrote letters. The Dreamers filled songs with feeling. Millennials shaped emotion through images and small posts.

Generation Alpha speaks through symbols. Quick signs. Faces that appear, vanish, and return. Sometimes a single image replaces an entire sentence. Their language moves fast. Understanding shifts with timing. A pause can say as much as a reply.

Speed can thin emotion until it becomes performance rather than understanding. They express themselves constantly, though they may rarely understand their own feelings.

"To feel quickly is human. To understand what you feel is divine." - *Santiago Dagon*

The work ahead is to teach reflection before reaction. Generation Alpha needs space to understand themselves before they turn their feelings into content.

Friendship In Real Time

Friendship once grew through long afternoons and unhurried talk. It formed in the rhythm of real companionship. Today it appears as a stream of notifications, small signs of closeness that travel through devices.

For the Generation Alpha child, response often equals connection. Silence can feel like disappearance. They may build real bonds through shared games and creative projects. They may form communities held together by play and shared purpose rather than geography.

Every friendship still hungers for connection that does not vanish when the screen goes dark. It longs for the unspoken things: the closeness of sitting nearby, the comfort of being known without words.

"A friend is not the one who replies, but the one whose calm still feels like company." - *Santiago Dagon*

The future of friendship for Generation Alpha may depend on balance. Genuine connection is not defined by constant interaction, but by steady, intentional care shown over time.

Identity In The Age Of Mirrors

The online environment now functions as both reflection and display. From the first shared photo or profile, a Generation Alpha child begins shaping how they are seen. That visibility can support exploration. It allows experimentation with interests, style, and voice. It can also put pressure on maintaining an image.

When feedback becomes constant, approval can start to feel like proof. Over time, that proof can shape self-perception. The curated image may begin to carry more influence than the person behind it.

As Santiago Dagon writes, **"When we stare too long at our reflection, we start to forget the one who is looking."**

For Generation Alpha, identity may need to stay flexible and real, not locked in or shaped for display. Growing up naturally involves change, mistakes, and trying again. It includes uncertain phases and ordinary days that are never shared online. Real growth happens in those unseen moments. Remembering that can help keep a young person's sense of self grounded in real life, not just in what is shown to others.

The Rise Of Digital Empathy

In the middle of nonstop information, something deeper is also developing. A new kind of empathy may be forming. Generation Alpha does not learn about distant events only through brief reports. They often see faces, hear voices, and watch events unfold as they happen. Because of this, what once felt far away can now feel close and personal.

When a destructive tropical storm impacts an Asian country, Generation Alpha children may encounter images and personal accounts within hours. Their response can be sincere and spontaneous. Compassion now travels through direct exposure rather than delayed reporting.

As Santiago Dagon writes, "**The heart does not care about geography. The map of caring has always lived within us.**"

This expanded awareness holds promise. It allows concern to extend beyond local boundaries. At the same time, continuous exposure to global hardship can weigh heavily. Emotional capacity has limits. Without balance, Generation Alpha feelings can lead to emotional exhaustion.

Privacy And Awareness

To earlier generations, privacy meant solitude. To Generation Alpha, privacy will mean choice. It will mean deciding what to share and what to protect.

Their lives begin under observation. Moments are recorded before memory can form. Transparency feels natural, even as the longing to be unseen remains.

"Only in darkness do stars remember how to shine."
- Santiago Dagon

For those guiding Generation Alpha, conversations about privacy take on deeper significance. Privacy is not only about security settings or passwords. It is about recognizing that some parts of life are not meant for public display.

In a culture that encourages sharing, it becomes important to recognize that withholding can also carry value. Certain experiences gain significance when they remain within a trusted circle. Not every emotion, achievement, or struggle needs an audience.

When Generation Alpha children learn that some moments are meant to be held rather than broadcast, they begin to see boundaries as protective rather than limiting. Connection is valued for its depth, not its visibility.

The Politics Of Belonging

Belonging is no longer defined only by location. Generation Alpha is growing up in networks where shared convictions often matter more than shared borders. Communities form around causes, values, and narratives. Young voices can join conversations that stretch across continents. Participation no longer waits for proximity.

As Santiago Dagon writes, **"We are no longer citizens of nations, but of the stories we choose to serve."**

This expanded freedom opens space for solidarity beyond geography. It also introduces complexity. When identity becomes tied primarily to group alignment, understanding can narrow. Shared purpose can unite. It can also divide when differences are framed as threats rather than perspectives.

The tension is not new, but the scale is. Digital connections amplifies both cooperation and conflict. For Generation Alpha, learning how to hold conviction without reducing others to opposition may shape the tone of public life in the years ahead. Standing for something does not require turning every disagreement into a boundary.

Loneliness In The Age Of Many Voices

The Generation Alpha world is based on connection. Connections have expanded in ways previous generations could not imagine. Messages move continuously. Group chats remain active. Notifications rarely pause. And still, many describe a persistent sense of isolation. Communication is constant, but depth can feel inconsistent. Words circulate widely. Understanding does not always follow.

As Santiago Dagon writes, **"Loneliness is not the absence of people. It is the absence of understanding."**

Generation Alpha is growing up in an environment built on fast communication. Because of that pace, meaningful conversation does not happen automatically. It takes intention. Listening can become scattered when attention is constantly pulled in different directions Speaking may begin to focus more on impressing others than on honestly expressing thoughts and feelings. And silence, instead of feeling natural, can seem awkward simply because it is rarely practiced.

Generation Alpha must learn that restoring intimacy may depend less on increasing communication and more on strengthening its quality. Listening without preparing a response. Speaking without curating an image. Remaining present when there is nothing to post. Real companionship develops when interaction moves beyond performance and into mutual recognition.

Family, Mentorship, And The Social Compass

The new social shift is not abstract. It shows up in living rooms and kitchens. Families now stretch across countries and time zones, meeting through small, illuminated screens. Grandparents read bedtime stories from thousands of miles away. Parents guide homework between meetings. Siblings exchange jokes from different rooms in the same house.

Technology supports connection across distance. It makes continuity possible in ways that were once unimaginable. At the same time, the deeper layers of wisdom still move through human example. A voice that slows to explain. A face that reacts with care. A conversation that adjusts in response to emotion.

As Santiago Dagon writes, **"Every family is a classroom of empathy. We teach love not by rules, but by rhythm."**

Generation Alpha children absorb more than instruction. They notice patterns. They observe how attention is given, how conflict is handled, and how time is shared. From those patterns, they begin to form an internal compass. Care is not automatic. It is practiced. And in that practice, values take shape.

From Connection To Deeper Relationship

Modern life is filled with communication. Conversations overlap. Devices illuminate rooms late into the evening. Information circulates continuously. Expression is constant. And beneath that activity, many people still long to feel understood.

Generation Alpha is growing up fluent in connection. What may require more attention is the depth within that connection. Listening can become reactive, focused on preparing a reply. There is another form of listening, one that absorbs context, tone, and feeling before responding.

As Santiago Dagon writes, **"True connection begins when words rest and awareness speaks."**

Contact is easy to establish. Kinship develops more slowly. It forms when two people recognize something real beneath the exchange and choose to engage it. A close relationship does not depend on volume or frequency. It depends on attention. In that kind of exchange, relationships move beyond interaction and become mutual understanding.

Closing Reflection

The social shift highlights something enduring. Every person seeks recognition. Not simply attention, but reflection that feels accurate. Generation Alpha is growing up in a world woven together by gestures and platforms. Their friendships may begin through screens, but the desire underneath them is not new. The need to belong has always been part of the human experience.

As Santiago Dagon writes, **"Connection is the new gravity of the universe. It draws us toward the realization that we were never separate."**

Digital networks can widen circles of interaction. What sustains those circles is something older. If Generation Alpha learns to form relationships with awareness, and to belong without dissolving their sense of self, the volume of the era does not have to define them.

Technology may shape the form of connection. Relationships themselves remain fundamental. It continues to anchor identity, purpose, and the experience of being human.

CHAPTER 6

THE EMOTIONAL CODE

"Emotion is the original intelligence. The rest are languages we built to explain it." - *Santiago Dagon*

The sections that follow examine how emotional life may take shape for Generation Alpha in a culture where feelings are expressed openly, tracked digitally, and shared across networks. Emotional experience is no longer private by default. It is often visible, labeled, and responded to in real time.

These pages consider emerging patterns connected to emotional awareness, empathy, public expression, and the development of an internal compass. The aim is to explore how Generation Alpha children growing up in this environment may understand their inner world, relate to the emotions of others, and form a sense of direction rooted in feeling as well as thought.

What follows is not a list of firm conclusions, but simple observations. The goal is not to predict, but to explore how emotional life may be changing and what those changes could mean.

The Pulse Beneath Progress

Each age moves to its own rhythm. For Generation Alpha, that rhythm feels continuous. Messages arrive at all hours. Images change in an instant. Stories begin before the last one finishes. Beneath this constant motion, the human heart keeps the same enduring pace it has held for centuries.

Emotion remains the compass that points thought in a direction. The modern world often treats it as something to tame or avoid, and every decision begins first as a feeling. An inaudible pull. A small ache. A moment of recognition.

Generation Alpha children are being raised in a world where empathy can be imitated by AI voices that speak smoothly and respond quickly, these artificial voices cannot feel what they reflect. Generation Alpha emotional development will depend less on the lessons they receive and more on the example they witness. They learn from adults who still know how to pause, how to breathe, and how to stay calm even in noise.

"We cannot teach children how to feel by telling them what to feel. They learn from the pauses between our words."
- Santiago Dagon

The Rise Of Emotional Awareness

For much of history, emotion lived behind walls of strength. People learned to push it aside rather than explore it. Now emotion has become something to notice, to name, and to share. This is progress. Human literacy is widening to include how people understand themselves, relate to others, and make thoughtful choices in a complex world.

Millennials pulled therapy into everyday conversation. Gen Z spoke openly about anxiety, identity, grief, and kindness. Generation Alpha will grow up hearing emotional vocabulary long before they master academic ones. Many schools already teach mindfulness, compassion, and the regulation of attention besides mathematics. This shift suggests that caring for the heart is as important as caring for the mind.

"The mind makes maps. The heart finds meaning."

- Santiago Dagon

Awareness, however, is only the first step. The deeper question for Generation Alpha becomes not Can I name this feeling? but Can I stay with it long enough to learn what it holds?

Feeling In Public

The Generation Alpha child lives within a world of open mirrors. Joy, confusion, frustration, and fear can be shared instantly. Emotion becomes a kind of performance. A moment that once belonged to the inner self can become a broadcast within seconds.

Attention begins to resemble affection. Affection begins to resemble validation. These currents shape the emotional instincts of childhood in ways earlier generations never faced.

"When we share pain to be seen, the pain forgets how to heal." *- Santiago Dagon*

Generation Alpha children will need private places where feelings can breathe before becoming content. A journal. A reinsuring talk at night. A walk without conversation. These simple moments restore the original purpose of emotion: not to entertain, but to guide.

Emotional Algorithms

Technology is increasingly designed to read emotional patterns. It analyzes pauses in typing, the music someone plays, the timing of responses, and the tone of language. From those traces, systems estimate mood. They adjust suggestions. They generate replies that sound supportive.

For Generation Alpha, these tools may feel responsive and personal. They can reply quickly and in ways that sound understanding. Still, this is pattern recognition, not relationship. Data can copy the shape of feeling, but it does not feel. Real connection comes from people who notice, respond, and share experience over time.

As Santiago Dagon writes, **"The machine may know how you feel, but only you can know what it means."**

For Generation Alpha, this distinction will matter. Emotional data may become part of everyday life. The question will not be whether systems can track feeling. It will be how individuals relate to that tracking.

Inner life carries nuance that cannot be reduced to metrics. Vulnerability involves context, history, and choice. When emotion becomes something measured, it risks becoming something managed. Preserving depth may require awareness of what is shared and what is held back. Some dimensions of feeling remain significant precisely because they are not optimized or analyzed.

The Language Of Empathy

Empathy functions as a kind of unseen framework within society. It allows one person to recognize that another carries experiences, memories, and emotions as real as their own. It tempers certainty. It introduces complexity. It reminds us that every life unfolds under different conditions.

Generation Alpha will not encounter empathy only through books or lessons. They will see expressions of suffering and support side by side on the same screen. They will witness generosity and hostility within a single scroll. Their emotional exposure may extend far beyond their immediate environment.

As Santiago Dagon writes, **"Empathy is not the act of feeling what others feel. It is remembering that they feel at all."**

Sustaining empathy requires balance. Continuous exposure to intense emotions can overwhelm the nervous system. Caring deeply without internal limits can lead to fatigue. The challenge is not reducing compassion. It is learning how to carry it in a way that remains sustainable. When empathy is supported by reflection and boundaries, it can motivate thoughtful action rather than emotional depletion.

Emotional Inheritance

Generation Alpha children will inherit more than physical traits. They absorb patterns. The tone used during conflict. The way attention is given or divided. The habit of listening fully or listening halfway. These repeated behaviors become templates long before a child can name them.

When a parent turns toward a device during conversation, the shift may register as distance, even when affection is unchanged. When a parent pauses and maintains eye contact, that pause communicates value beyond words. Children learn relational habits through observation as much as instruction.

As Santiago Dagon writes, **"The child does not remember what we said. They remember how we looked while listening."**

The significance of these patterns is not fixed. They can evolve. A sincere apology models accountability. A slower response during tension demonstrates regulation. A moment of focused attention communicates value. Over time, these small adjustments influence the emotional blueprint that moves from one generation to the next.

The Inner Landscape

The external world continues to accelerate. Messages multiply. Visual stimuli compete for attention. At the same time, the internal world remains expansive and largely unseen. For Generation Alpha, one of the most significant developments may not be centered on devices at all. It may involve understanding their own interior life. The part of the self that observes, imagines, questions, and feels.

Practices such as reflective writing, artistic expression, time in natural settings, or contemplative stillness can support that awareness. These experiences do not compete with technology. They offer a different dimension of engagement. They create space for interpretation rather than reaction.

As Santiago Dagon writes**, "To know yourself is to hold a conversation with silence."**

Developing familiarity with one's inner landscape contributes to resilience. It strengthens the ability to pause before responding. It builds a reference point that does not depend on external validation. In a culture shaped by algorithms and acceleration, internal clarity becomes a stabilizing force.

The Science Of Feeling

Research in neuroscience increasingly confirms something long observed in literature and lived experience. Emotional response often precedes conscious thought. The body registers change before the mind assigns explanation. Heart rate shifts. Muscles tighten. Attention narrows or widens. Interpretation follows sensation.

Learning is shaped by this sequence. A regulated nervous system supports curiosity and memory. A heightened stress response can limit both. The connection between emotion and cognition is not theoretical. It is biological.

As Santiago Dagon writes, **"Emotional maturity is not the absence of storms. It is learning to sail while they pass."**

When children are taught that feelings function as information rather than danger, their sensitivity becomes an asset. Emotions signal values, needs, and boundaries. Recognizing those signals does not eliminate discomfort. It builds skill in moving through it.

This capacity to notice emotion, interpret it, and respond with intention may become one of the defining competencies of the coming decades. Emotional agility supports adaptation. It allows individuals to experience intensity without being overtaken by it.

Healing Through Expression

Every generation has experiences that were difficult to name in their time. Generation Alpha is entering a culture more willing to acknowledge emotional struggle openly. Language around mental health is more accessible. Creative outlets are widely available.

Music, visual art, writing, and digital creation provide avenues for translating internal experience into form. When emotion is given structure, it becomes easier to examine. What feels overwhelming in silence can become clearer when expressed.

As Santiago Dagon writes, **"Healing is not forgetting what hurt. It is learning to live gently beside it."**

Expression does not erase pain. It allows it to be processed. When children are encouraged to communicate honestly, whether through conversation or creativity, they develop tools for integration rather than suppression. Art, in this sense, becomes more than decoration. It becomes a method of understanding. Through expression, emotion finds movement. And in that movement, healing becomes possible.

The New Compass

Emotion has always influenced decision making, even when it operates beneath conscious awareness. Technology can process data and optimize outcomes, but it does not experience attachment, loss, or care. It calculates. It does not feel.

As societies continue to automate tasks and systems, the qualities that remain distinctly human become more visible. Emotional intelligence, once considered secondary to analytical ability, is increasingly recognized as central to leadership, collaboration, and ethical judgment.

As Santiago Dagon writes, **"When all else can be automated, love will be the last true intelligence."**

The ability to reflect inwardly may shape how outward systems are built. Individuals who understand their own motivations and emotional patterns are better positioned to design structures that account for human complexity.

If Generation Alpha develops this depth of awareness, innovation may not be defined solely by efficiency or scale. It may also be guided by compassion, perspective, and an understanding of the human experience at its core.

Closing Reflection

We are raising the first generation to grow up where emotional life and digital systems intersect daily. Their decisions will not separate feelings from technology. They will learn to integrate both.

If the adults around them model reflection and responsibility, empathy may find its way into the structures they create. If emotional depth is overlooked, innovation could move forward without a clear human center.

As Santiago Dagon writes, **"The evolution of humanity is not from ignorance to knowledge, but from indifference to empathy."**

The patterns children internalize now may influence how future systems are designed and governed. Emotional awareness may become part of the underlying framework guiding progress. The question is not whether technology will advance. It will. The question is what values will accompany that advancement.

For Generation Alpha, feelings are not distractions from growth. They are signals. They provide information about connection, impact, and responsibility. When interpreted thoughtfully, they become orientation points. In that sense, emotion is not noise. It is direction.

CHAPTER 7

VALUES IN FLUX

"Values are not rules written in stone. They are rivers, forever seeking the sea of meaning." - *Santiago Dagon*

The sections that follow look at how values may be taking shape within Generation Alpha. These children are growing up in a setting defined by global connection and constant exposure to differing viewpoints. In that environment, moral awareness does not disappear. It adapts.

The themes ahead explore patterns related to truth, integrity, shifting moral frameworks, ethical questions surrounding artificial intelligence, and the courage required to care in public spaces. Each topic reflects tensions already visible in daily life.

What follows is not a forecast or a verdict. It is an exploration of developments already unfolding. These brief reflections consider how moral and emotional understanding may evolve within a culture shaped by speed, visibility, and continuous exchange.

Think of these ideas as reflections to consider. Pay attention to what feels familiar in your own life. Look for these patterns in the children you see each day, whether at home, in school, or in the digital spaces they move through.

The Shifting Ground Beneath Certainty

Every generation assumes that its moral framework will endure. History suggests otherwise. Cultural norms evolve. Language shifts. What once changed slowly now transforms rapidly, amplified by digital networks before reflection has time to catch up.

Generation Alpha is living within this accelerated exchange. Moral understanding may not arrive as a single inherited code. It may develop through exposure to multiple cultures, viewpoints, and interpretations encountered daily. Their framework of right and wrong could resemble a mosaic, assembled from varied influences rather than carved from one source.

In that environment, context gains importance. Conviction may coexist with empathy. Listening becomes part of moral practice, not a substitute for it.

As Santiago Dagon writes, **"Certainty is the comfort of yesterday. Wisdom begins when we can listen to tomorrow."**

The main challenge for this generation may not be choosing between clear opposites. Instead, it may be learning how to think carefully. When many voices claim to define what is true, the ability to question, compare, and decide wisely becomes important. Moral growth may depend less on strict rules and more on the ability to work through complicated ideas with care.

The Collapse Of Moral Distance

Visibility has expanded in ways few imagined. A child in Hanoi can follow a flood in Brazil, a protest in New York, or an act of generosity in Thailand before the day ends. Events once filtered through layers of distance now appear directly and immediately.

This proximity changes moral perception. Separation feels less convincing when faces and stories are constantly present. Compassion can extend far beyond local surroundings. At the same time, continuous exposure places pressure on emotional capacity.

Alpha children may sense responsibility for situations far outside their influence. They may absorb conflict without the context needed to interpret it fully.

As Santiago Dagon writes, **"Awareness is a gift until it becomes an avalanche."**

Moral development may depend on balance. Knowing when to engage, when to reflect, and when to step back becomes part of ethical growth. Empathy that is paced thoughtfully can move from immediate reaction toward sustained responsibility.

The Rise Of Moral Imagination

In past generations, ideas about right and wrong came largely from family life, religious traditions, and close-knit communities. Generation Alpha will still encounter those influences, but their field of exposure is much wider. Through stories, interactive media, and virtual environments, they can step into perspectives far removed from their own daily lives.

Imagination becomes part of moral formation. When a child considers another person's experience, empathy can expand beyond immediate surroundings.

As Santiago Dagon writes, **"To imagine another's life is the first act of moral awakening."**

Digital spaces can make it hard to tell the difference between what is real and what is carefully staged. Images and stories can look authentic while leaving out important context or facts. As a result, strong emotions can be stirred before there is a full understanding of what is actually happening.

Moral imagination is powerful, but it needs a steady foundation. When it is guided by careful thinking, it deepens empathy. When it is driven only by dramatic images or reactions, it can lead to confusion. For Generation Alpha, the challenge may be learning how to let imagination expand perspective without losing the ability to think clearly and question what they see.

Truth In The Age Of Filters

There was a time when information was limited. Access required effort. Today the challenge is the opposite. Facts, opinions, images, and interpretations circulate at extraordinary speed. Volume increases. Clarity does not always follow.

The distinction between authentic and fabricated content grows more complex. Synthetic voices can sound human. Artificial faces can appear credible. Stories can be constructed with persuasive detail. Emotional reaction can be triggered before verification takes place.

As Santiago Dagon writes, **"When facts multiply, faith in perception must deepen."**

For Generation Alpha, understanding truth may rely less on storing facts and more on learning how to examine and question information. The ability to check sources and compare evidence will matter. So will the habit of thinking carefully and ethically about what is being presented. Not every powerful story is honest.

In this environment, clear answers may not always be easy to find. Steadiness over time becomes important. Does the information match reliable evidence? Does it remain consistent when looked at closely? Truth may not always feel obvious, but it often becomes clearer when facts, experience, and integrity align.

Redefining Integrity

Integrity was once described as doing what is right when no one is watching. In a networked culture, observation is more common. Actions are recorded. Words can be shared widely. Visibility becomes part of daily life.

This environment can influence behavior in different ways. It can produce caution driven by fear of exposure. It can also create accountability that encourages responsibility.

As Santiago Dagon writes, **"Integrity is what we do when we know the world is watching, and what we still do when it is not."**

For Generation Alpha, integrity may be understood less as flawlessness and more as consistency. Mistakes will occur in public and private. What may matter most is response. A willingness to acknowledge error. A willingness to repair.

In that pattern, integrity becomes less about perfection and more about alignment. Returning to truth repeatedly. Acting with consideration in ordinary moments. Over time, those repeated choices form character.

The Marketplace Of Morals

Ethical language now circulates alongside products and platforms. Companies highlight social commitments. Campaigns align with causes. Algorithms amplify strong reactions, often favoring outrage because it travels quickly. Justice can become a slogan as easily as a conviction.

This blending of commerce and ethics carries both potential and risk. Public attention can bring awareness to important issues. At the same time, repeated exposure to packaged virtue can blur the line between commitment and marketing.

As Santiago Dagon writes, **"Goodness cannot be advertised. It must be lived enough to be felt."**

For Generation Alpha, an important skill may be learning how to tell the difference between how something looks and what it truly stands for. Being visible or popular does not automatically mean something is honest or meaningful. Speaking loudly or often does not make an idea sincere. What matters most is whether actions match values consistently over time, especially when no one is watching.

The Moral Imprint Of AI

Artificial intelligence is becoming part of the background architecture of daily life. It influences what children read, watch, purchase, and sometimes even who they meet. Recommendations are shaped by data patterns. Choices are nudged by unseen code.

These systems do not emerge from neutrality. They are built by people, trained in human history, and shaped by existing assumptions. If bias exists in society, it can be reflected in the systems that learn from it. Blind spots do not disappear when they are digitized. They can become embedded.

As Santiago Dagon writes, **"We must build intelligence that remembers the heartbeat."**

For Generation Alpha, ethical awareness will extend beyond personal behavior. It will include understanding how tools are designed and how those tools influence outcomes. The responsibility is not only individual. It is structural.

The coming decades may require moral frameworks that address both human intention and technological design.

Conscience cannot remain separate from innovation. The systems that guide decisions will increasingly need principles that reflect shared human values and diverse perspectives.

Tradition In Translation

Longstanding traditions are unlikely to vanish. They tend to adapt. Practices once expressed in formal language may be reinterpreted in contemporary terms. Rituals may shift form while preserving intentions. Dialogue may replace debate in some spaces.

As Santiago Dagon writes, **"Tradition survives not by resisting time, but by finding new forms for its fire."**

Generation Alpha is growing up with access to spiritual and philosophical teachings from many cultures at once. Exposure to multiple traditions may encourage comparison, blending, and reinterpretation. For some, identity may be shaped less by exclusive allegiance and more by shared themes across traditions.

This does not require abandoning heritage. It may involve translating it. Values such as reverence, gratitude, and compassion can appear in varied forms while pointing toward similar principles. The question becomes how inherited wisdom is carried forward in a language that resonates within a connected world.

The Ethics Of Earth

Few generations have entered childhood with such widespread awareness of environmental strain. News of climate patterns, species decline, and resource pressure appears early and often. For Generation Alpha, these realities may register less as distant policy debates and more as conditions shaping daily life.

As Santiago Dagon writes, **"The planet does not belong to us. We are shaped by its breathing."**

Exposure to ecological concerns at a young age may broaden the scope of moral consideration. The circle of concern may extend beyond human communities to include landscapes, waterways, and nonhuman life. Environmental care may be framed less as optional activism and more as shared responsibility.

In that shift, stewardship becomes relational rather than charitable. Protection of ecosystems is not an abstract ideal. It reflects recognition of interdependence. Survival, health, and stability are understood as connected across species and regions.

How this generation interprets that awareness may influence not only environmental policy, but cultural values about consumption, growth, and responsibility in the decades ahead.

The Courage To Care

At the center of many moral decisions is something uncomplicated but demanding: the choice to care. Indifference often requires less effort. Attention can be diverted. Discomfort can be avoided. Caring asks for engagement.

Generation Alpha will not lack access to issues or causes. Information will reach them without effort. The challenge may lie in sustaining concern without becoming overwhelmed or detached. Attention is constantly pulled in different directions. Holding onto what matters requires intention.

As Santiago Dagon writes, **"Courage is not the absence of fear. It is the refusal to stop caring."**

Moral formation rarely depends on grand gestures alone. It is shaped in daily interactions. A measured tone during conflict. An apology offered sincerely. Fairness practiced in small decisions. Consideration shown in routine moments.

Alpha children observe these patterns. They form expectations about what care looks like. The moral environment they inherit will be influenced as much by consistent examples as by public debate.

Closing Reflection

Shifts in values do not automatically indicate decline. They often reflect adaptation. As cultures evolve, moral language adjusts to new circumstances. The core questions remain familiar: How do we live well together? What do we owe to one another?

For Generation Alpha, ethical understanding may feel less imposed and more discovered. Exposure to diverse perspectives encourages evaluation rather than simple acceptance.

Awareness, connection, and discernment become part of moral formation.

As Santiago Dagon writes, **"Morality is the art of remembering that we belong to everything we touch."**

If this generation learns to pair independence with respect, individuality with consideration, and influence with responsibility, change need not destabilize them. It can clarify priorities.

In that process, morality does not harden into rigidity, nor does it dissolve into confusion. It adapts. It remains responsive to context while anchored in shared human concerns. Through ongoing reflection and lived experience, ethical understanding continues to take shape.

CHAPTER 8

EDUCATION REINVENTED

"Education was never meant to fill the mind. It was meant to free it." - *Santiago Dagon*

The sections that follow explore how education may evolve for Generation Alpha. Learning is already expanding beyond traditional walls, shaped by digital access, cultural exchange, and shifting expectations about what it means to be educated.

These pages consider emerging patterns related to the migration of classrooms, new teaching approaches, the teacher's evolving role, technology as a learning partner, education of the whole child, the decline of rigid standardization, lifelong learning as a way of living, the global classroom, and the future of wisdom itself.

What follows is not a blueprint for reform. It is an examination of trends already visible. Each theme offers a brief reflection on how learning, development, and growth may unfold within a culture defined by connection and rapid change.

In each section notice what resonates with your own experience. Consider how these patterns show up in the children you teach, guide, or care for. The purpose is not prediction. It is awareness of how education may transform in the New Humanity Shift.

From Classrooms To Tomorrow's World

For generations, learning took place inside defined spaces. Rows of desks. Chalkboard at the front of the room. Schedules that organized the day. These structures reflected the needs of their time. They prepared students for stable roles within stable systems. Change occurred, but often at a measured pace.

Today, information evolves rapidly. New research appears daily. Industries transform within a decade. A printed text can feel outdated before it is fully circulated. The framework that once contained knowledge now struggles to keep up with its expansion.

Learning has begun to move beyond fixed boundaries. It happens across platforms, in communities, through collaboration and self-directed exploration. It is less contained by walls and more shaped by networks.

As Santiago Dagon writes, **"The classroom was once a room. Now it is the world itself."**

Generation Alpha is entering an imaginative flowing environment. They may not receive a single roadmap. They will encounter movement and change as constants. In that setting, the role of educators' shifts. The emphasis moves from delivering answers to cultivating inquiry.

The enduring lesson may not be mastery of fixed content, but the ability to ask worthwhile questions and keep learning long after formal instruction ends.

The Death Of Memorization

There was a period when education centered on recall. To remember accurately was to demonstrate mastery. Repetition confirmed competence. Memory functioned as a primary measure of success.

Today, much of that recall has shifted outward. Digital systems store and retrieve information instantly. Search tools deliver data within seconds. Facts are no longer scarce resources guarded by textbooks. They are widely accessible.

As Santiago Dagon writes, **"Memory is useful, but purpose is enduring."**

The New Humanity Shift is changing what learning looks like for Generation Alpha. Information is easy to store and access through devices, so memorizing facts matters less than before. What matters more is knowing how to understand that information, connect ideas, and use them wisely. Students are being asked not just to repeat what they hear, but to think critically, make sense of patterns, and apply learning to real situations.

Generation Alpha will likely be expected to do what automated systems cannot do. To interpret context. To weigh consequences. To recognize ethical dimensions within knowledge. In this environment, the mind functions less as an archive and more as a workshop, shaping raw information into understanding and judgment.

Learning By Doing, Learning By Being

When curiosity guides the development, learning regains momentum. Future classrooms may look less like lecture halls and more like studios, Gardens, and collaborative workspaces. Students may experiment before they define terms. They may build before they describe.

As Santiago Dagon writes, **"We remember best not what we are told, but what we discover with our own hands."**

Experience tends to anchor knowledge more firmly than repetition alone. When children engage directly with materials, ideas, or environments, understanding becomes embodied. It moves beyond abstraction.

In this setting, mistakes take on a different role. They become part of the process rather than a final judgment. Attempting, adjusting, and trying again becomes expected. Failure signals participation, not inadequacy.

Learning through action and reflection reconnects education with daily life. It invites students to integrate thought, creativity, and resilience. Over time, knowledge grows not only through instruction, but through lived experience.

The Teacher's New Role

The image of a teacher standing at the front of the room as the sole authority is gradually shifting. Access to information is no longer confined to one voice. As a result, the teacher's position is changing from primary source to active guide.

Instruction increasingly resembles dialogue. Questions move in both directions. Engagement matters as much as content delivery. Expertise remains important, but it is paired with attentiveness and adaptability.

As Santiago Dagon writes, **"A true teacher does not give answers. They awaken the courage to ask."**

In this evolving model, the classroom feels less like a formal ritual and more like a shared space of inquiry. Teachers listen with intention. They move alongside students as ideas develop. Authority is expressed through clarity and example rather than distance.

Learning becomes collaborative. It unfolds through conversation, experimentation, and reflection. In that exchange, both student and teacher participate in growth.

Technology As Partner, Not Replacement

Digital tools now assist learning in ways that once felt visionary. They translate languages instantly. They adjust lessons to an individual pace. They recognize patterns and suggest next steps with impressive precision. For many students, these systems function as daily tutors.

At the same time, digital tools remain mechanisms. They process information. They do not feel curiosity. They cannot offer reassurance drawn from human experience, empathy, and shared struggles.

As Santiago Dagon writes, **"Let technology be the map, not the journey."**

When integrated thoughtfully, technology can reduce repetitive tasks and free educators to focus on mentoring, discussion, and individual support. It can expand access and personalize instruction.

When used without reflection, however, learning can become overly quantified. Metrics can overshadow understanding. Progress can be measured in data points rather than growth.

The essential question is not whether technology belongs in education. It does. The question is how it is positioned. When tools support human guidance rather than replace it, learning retains depth and relational context.

Education Of The Whole Child

For a long time, formal education prioritized intellectual performance. Academic achievement was measured primarily through cognitive outcomes. Imagination, physical well-being, and emotional development were often treated as secondary.

Generation Alpha may question that separation. Growing up in an interconnected world, they experience thought and feeling as intertwined. Learning that engages only the analytical dimension can feel incomplete.

As Santiago Dagon writes, **"Knowledge without empathy is like a flame without warmth."**

Educational environments may increasingly integrate reflection alongside reasoning. Creative expression may accompany technical skill. Physical movement and emotional intelligence may sit beside mathematics and language study.

In that futuristic outlook, schools become places that cultivate growth rather than simply evaluate performance. Achievement is not defined solely by comparison. It is also measured by contribution, collaboration, and the ability to apply knowledge with awareness.

The End Of Standardization

Standardized testing was introduced to promote consistency and fairness. Over time, it has also contributed to fatigue and comparison. Students develop at different paces, with varied strengths and contexts. Measuring them on a single scale can overlook that diversity.

Generation Alpha may challenge systems that reduce growth to uniform metrics. Exposure to personalized technology has shaped expectations. Many Alpha children are accustomed to adaptive environments. In that perspective, fixed benchmarks can feel disconnected from individual development.

As Santiago Dagon writes, **"There is no standard for wonder. Each mind blooms in its own rhythm."**

Assessment may gradually shift from ranking toward reflection. Rather than focusing solely on retention, evaluation could include interpretation, creativity, and self-awareness. The central question moves from academic scores alone to insight: What was understood? What was created? How has perspective changed?

When assessment broadens in this way, measurement becomes less about comparison and more about growth.

Lifelong Learning As Lifestyle

Education is no longer confined to childhood or early adulthood. In a culture defined by instant change, skills evolve, industries shift, and new knowledge emerges continuously. Reinvention becomes part of ordinary daily life. Learning is less about completing a program and more about staying responsive to the world.

As Santiago Dagon writes, **"The educated are not those who have finished learning, but those who have learned how to begin again."**

In this landscape, generational boundaries begin to blur. Older adults return to studying new fields. Young people introduce tools and perspectives unfamiliar to their elders. Classrooms include multiple ages, both formally and informally.

Learning becomes reciprocal. Teachers adapt alongside students. Students contribute insights shaped by their lived experiences. Knowledge flows in more than one direction.

Over time, education shifts from a defined stage of life to continuous practice. Curiosity becomes less an academic requirement and more a way of engaging with change.

Learning Through Purpose

Motivation is evolving. Achievement still carries value, but purpose increasingly shapes engagement. Many young Alpha learners ask not only how to complete a task, but why it matters. Relevance influences attention.

Generation Alpha is likely to seek connections between knowledge and lived experiences. Information that contributes to community, environment, or shared well-being may feel more compelling than material pursued solely for advancement.

As Santiago Dagon writes, **"Purpose is the gravity that keeps learning from drifting away."**

When learning aligns with contribution, engagement deepens. Projects tied to real world impact tend to sustain interest. Curiosity gains direction when it is connected to service.

Educational environments that integrate purpose alongside skill development may support both competence and character. In that alignment, learning becomes more than preparation. It becomes participation in a broader human context.

The Global Classroom

Cultural boundaries feel less settled than they once did. Translation tools operate instantly. Collaborative projects span continents. Students exchange ideas across time zones as part of ordinary learning. The world increasingly functions as a shared educational space.

As Santiago Dagon writes, **"Every culture holds a piece of the world's wisdom. Education is the act of listening to them all."**

Access alone does not guarantee understanding. Exposure is immediate. Comprehension takes time. Cultural context, history, and nuances require attention beyond a brief exchange.

This environment invites humility. No single tradition carries the entire narrative. Collaboration becomes more productive than rivalry when diverse perspectives are treated as contributions rather than threats.

Learning across cultures can expand awareness and refine judgment. When approached with respect, it reinforces the idea that wisdom is distributed rather than centralized. In that recognition, education becomes both broader and deeper.

The Future Of Wisdom

Information continues to expand at an extraordinary rate. Data accumulates. Research advances. Access improves. And still, wisdom does not increase automatically with knowledge. The two are related, but they are not identical.

Wisdom integrates intellect with conscience. It considers consequence alongside capability. It asks not only what can be done, but what should be done. In a culture driven by innovation, that distinction becomes increasingly important.

As Santiago Dagon writes, **"The mind seeks mastery. The heart seeks meaning. Wisdom begins where they meet."**

Preparing Generation Alpha for constant change may depend less on teaching every possible subject and more on helping them develop discernment. This includes learning how to reflect on their own thoughts and feelings, listening carefully to others, and pause before reacting. These skills help children make sense of fast-moving information rather than feel overwhelmed by it.

These abilities are rarely listed on a syllabus, but they influence decisions throughout life. In a world where content updates nonstop, habits of thoughtful attention may offer the most reliable form of guidance.

Closing Reflection

Education has often been described as a ladder to climb, step by step toward achievement. It may be closer to a horizon, something that continues to expand as one approaches it. Learning was never meant to end at a final rung of the bell or graduation. It was meant to widen perspective over time.

Generation Alpha will inherit tools of remarkable sophistication. Access to information will rarely be the limiting factor. The deeper inheritance may be awareness, the capacity to apply knowledge with discernment and responsibility.

As Santiago Dagon writes, **"The future of learning is not technology. It is tenderness."**

When intelligence is joined with empathy, and curiosity is balanced by respect for complexity, education aligns with its broader purpose. Reinvention becomes less urgent when intention is clear.

At its core, learning is not simply preparation for work. It is participation in the ongoing development of character and understanding. Across a lifetime, education unfolds not only as skill acquisition, but as the gradual shaping of wisdom.

CHAPTER 9

PLAY, SPORTS, AND HOBBIES

"Play is not escape from life. It is the rehearsal for living it well." - *Santiago Dagon*

The sections that follow explore how play, sports, and hobbies may evolve for Generation Alpha. Recreation is no longer separate from technology, identity, or community. It reflects broader cultural shifts in attention, movement, and purpose.

These pages consider emerging patterns connected to the nature of play, the digital playground, renewed awareness of the body's need for movement, the evolution of competition, creativity as play, the role of nature in recreation, a renewed interest in hobbies, the importance of rest and recovery, and the place of reflective or spiritual practice within daily life.

What follows examines patterns that can already be seen taking shape. Each theme reflects on how recreation and personal expression are evolving within a culture defined by constant connection and accelerating change.

Read these insights as thoughtful observations. Notice where they resonate with your own experiences and how they appear in the lives of the children around you. The aim is to deepen awareness of how play and recreation are shifting, and how those shifts may influence emotional and social development in the years to come.

The Nature Of Play

Long before children can identify letters or understand directions, they begin by exploring. They stretch their arms, reach for objects, stack what they find, fall over, and try again. Play becomes an early form of learning. Through it, children test boundaries, negotiate roles, and discover cause and effect. Cooperation emerges without formal teaching. Resilience forms through repeated attempts. Empathy appears when play involves others.

Generation Alpha is growing up with two environments for play. One is physical, shaped by outdoor space, movement, and direct contact with materials. The other is digital, built from interactive platforms and shared virtual spaces. Both invite imagination. A child may climb a tree in the afternoon and construct a digital model in the evening.

As Santiago Dagon writes, **"The instinct to play is older than thought itself. It is the soul remembering how to grow."**

Across both environments, the underlying function of play remains consistent. It supports experimentation. It creates room for collaboration. It introduces belonging through shared experience. Play is not a distraction from development. It is one of its earliest and most enduring forms.

The Digital Playground

Play now extends into spaces that are not bound by parks, sports fields, and gymnasiums. Alpha children gather in the virtual metaverse, speaking through stereo headsets, represented by avatars, solving challenges together, and designing entire new worlds. Their imagination moves between physical and digital settings with little friction.

From an adult perspective, this form of play can raise concern. For many Alpha children, however, these platforms function as social spaces. Teams collaborate. Roles are negotiated. Leadership emerges during shared challenges. Bonds form through cooperative effort.

As Santiago Dagon writes, **"Imagination is the new arena. The games we play shape the kind of world we build."**

Digital play carries advantages. It also introduces risk. Continuous engagement can narrow attention. Achievement systems can shift focus from enjoyment to performance pressure.

The key may lie in rhythm rather than rejection. Moving between environments. Stepping outside. Reconnecting with physical sensation and unstructured time. When play remains varied and intentional, it supports growth rather than replacing it.

Rediscovering The Body

In an era shaped by screens and extended sitting, physical movement can become secondary. The body, however, continues to require physical activity. Running, climbing, stretching, and even falling provide feedback that no device can replicate. Through movement, children experience coordination, balance, and spatial awareness. They learn the limits and capacities of their own strength.

As Santiago Dagon writes, **"The body is a wise teacher. It reminds the mind that freedom is not a download. It is breath."**

Sports remain a central language of childhood. Sports communicate teamwork, discipline, and perseverance without lengthy explanation. In the coming years, some activities may blend physical exertion with digital enhancement. Others will retain traditional forms. Yoga and dance may share equal cultural space with robotics clubs and esports leagues.

The emphasis may gradually move from narrow definitions of victory toward broader measures of wellbeing. Physical activity supports emotional regulation, social connection, and vitality. In the New Humanity Shift, movement is not only physical exercise or competition. It becomes restoration.

The Play Of The Mind

Play does not belong only to the body. It also unfolds in imagination. Generation Alpha is growing up with tools that allow ideas to take shape quickly. A gesture can sketch a magical landscape. A touch can layer sound into composition. Stories can be designed, edited, and shared without traditional materials.

As Santiago Dagon writes, **"To play with ideas is to practice the art of becoming."**

In this setting, hobbies often merge learning and enjoyment. Creative exploration may involve coding, digital art, music production, storytelling, or design. The boundary between recreation and skill development becomes less distinct.

When children experiment with ideas in this way, they are not only producing content. They are refining perspective. The act of shaping an idea into form strengthens attention and interpretation. Play becomes a method of understanding, and imagination becomes a pathway to growth.

The Evolution Of Competition

Competition is unlikely to disappear. It has long motivated effort, focus, and discipline. What may change is how it is understood. For many young people, the emphasis may shift from defeating an opponent to refining personal capacity.

As Santiago Dagon writes, **"To compete with others is to sharpen the ego. To compete with oneself is to polish the soul."**

Team sports will continue, adapting to new formats and expectations. Collaboration and fairness may matter as much as performance outcomes. Recognition will still matter. Achievement will still be celebrated.

At the same time, growth may become a primary metric. Improvement over time. Commitment to practice. Resilience after setback. In this framing, competition becomes less about comparison and more about development. It remains challenging, but it also becomes reflective, grounded in personal progress as much as external reward.

Creativity As Play

For many children in Generation Alpha, creativity will not feel separate from daily life. It will move through how they communicate, solve problems, and explore identity. Drawing, composing, designing, and recording may arise from curiosity rather than performance. Creation becomes a way for Generation Alpha to understand themselves and the world more fully, shaping experience into meaning through what they make, imagine, and share.

As Santiago Dagon writes, **"Creation is how the soul breathes."**

For Generation Alpha children, creative work does more than build technique. It strengthens patience as they return to an idea and try again. It teaches revision as a natural part of growth, not a sign of failure. It encourages honest expression, helping them translate feelings and thoughts into something visible.

Developing a craft takes time because real creation rarely happens in a single attempt. An idea begins loosely. It shifts as the child experiments, adjusts, and revises. For Generation Alpha children, who are growing up in an environment of instant feedback and rapid results, this slower rhythm can feel unfamiliar at first. Growth occurs within that stretch of time.

When a child redraws a line, rewrites a sentence, rebuilds a structure that has collapsed, or practices a piece of music repeatedly, something steady forms beneath the surface. Attention strengthens. Frustration becomes manageable. Small improvements become visible. They begin to understand that quality is shaped through repetition and care.

In a world that moves quickly, the time required for developing a craft offers balance. It teaches that not everything meaningful arrives instantly. Creative practice can alter tempo. It introduces duration. Ideas are shaped, reconsidered, and refined. In that extended rhythm, understanding deepens. Creativity becomes not only output, but reflection.

The Role Of Nature In Play

Long before organized sports or digital platforms existed, children learned through interaction with the natural world. The sound of moving water, the shift of light across the ground, the scent that follows rain. These early sensory experiences shape perception and curiosity.

As Santiago Dagon writes, **"The earth was our first playground. It is still the only one that can teach reverence."**

Even in highly connected environments, interest in nature persists. Families continue to seek parks, trails, and open space. Educators incorporate outdoor learning where possible. Direct contact with soil, wind, and seasonal change offers a form of grounding that complements digital engagement.

For Generation Alpha, time outdoors may function not as nostalgia, but as balance. Collecting stones, observing insects, or climbing uneven terrain introduces unpredictability and physical awareness. In those moments, recreation connects with perspective. Joy is discovered not only in constructed environments, but in the world that existed long before them.

The Hobby Renaissance

Hobbies may regain significance as spaces of voluntary engagement. Baking, Gardening, knitting, repairing bicycles, building models, flying drones. These activities are not driven by grades or performance metrics. They are chosen. That choice changes the experience.

When time is spent on a task for its own sake, attention shifts. The pace slows. Repetition becomes practice rather than pressure. Satisfaction comes from process rather than outcome.

As Santiago Dagon writes, **"When we do something only for love, we restore balance to a world obsessed with outcome."**

Hobbies cultivate focus. They introduce humility when a project does not work the first time. They build patience through incremental progress.

For Generation Alpha, personal pursuits may serve as counterweights to constant urgency. They offer intervals where curiosity leads without external demand. In those spaces, learning remains personal and self-directed, shaped by interest rather than expectation.

Play, Rest, And The Rhythm Of Joy

Joy cannot be maintained through effort alone. It depends on regular moments of rest and renewal. In many modern environments, children are encouraged to stay productive and busy, while rest is treated as optional or secondary. Over time, this imbalance can drain attention and dull creativity, making it harder for young people to stay curious, engaged, and emotionally present.

As Santiago Dagon writes, **"Rest is the invisible half of play."**

For Generation Alpha, rest may need to be understood as an active element of well-being rather than an absence of activity. Unscheduled time. Periods without screens. Moments when thought can wander without direction.

When the nervous system resets, imagination regains clarity. Play becomes exploratory rather than compulsive. Creativity returns with renewed focus.

Rhythm shapes growth. Effort needs space to breathe. Action benefits from reflection. When action and rest move in balance, joy does not fade; it renews itself.

Play As Spiritual Practice

At a deeper level, play can take on a reflective quality. When a child becomes absorbed in movement, music, or creation, attention narrows and awareness sharpens. Effort and enjoyment merge. The experience feels immersive rather than distracting.

As Santiago Dagon writes, **"Play is prayer without words."**

For Generation Alpha, spirituality may not always center on formal rituals. It may appear in states of flow, in focused creativity, or in moments of awe. Wonder becomes a point of connection.

In these experiences, awareness heightens without force. Joy and attentiveness coincide. Play, in this sense, is not separate from purpose. It becomes a way of engaging life fully, with curiosity and openness.

Closing Reflection

Play, sport, and creative expression are often treated as breaks from serious work. In reality, they shape personal development in ways formal instruction cannot. They teach cooperation, adaptability, and emotional regulation. They loosen rigidity and reintroduce flexibility into thinking and feeling.

As Santiago Dagon writes**, "A world that forgets how to play forgets how to love."**

Joy carries intelligence. It invites connection. It eases division. When children engage in play, they rehearse empathy, negotiation, and resilience without labeling it as such.

Generation Alpha may grow up integrating purpose with recreation rather than separating the two. Movement may coexist with reflection. Creativity may exist alongside responsibility. In that integration, human development appears less fragmented.

Through these patterns, the practice of being human may take on renewed balance. The New Humanity Shift is not driven solely by output or achievement, but informed by engagement, curiosity, and purpose.

CHAPTER 10

THE FAMILY ECOSYSTEM

"Family is not a structure. It is a rhythm of care that keeps repeating, no matter how the world rearranges its walls." - *Santiago Dagon*

Every generation grows within a distinctive environment. Climate shapes crops. Culture shapes children. For Generation Alpha, that environment includes rapid technological expansion, evolving social norms, and a widening definition of belonging. Beneath these changes, the family remains the first system they encounter.

The home is more than a residence. It functions as an emotional training ground, a relational network, and an interpretive lens through which the wider world is understood. Within it, children begin forming ideas about trust, authority, identity, responsibility, and care. They observe how adults handle tension. They notice how affection is expressed. They learn what conflict means and whether it can be repaired.

Families today operate within layered realities. Physical and digital life intertwine. Extended relatives may live across continents and remain present through daily communication. Support systems expand beyond geography. Values evolve in conversation with culture rather than standing apart from it. The structure of family has diversified; its influence continues to shape how emotional development unfolds.

Generation Alpha is growing up in a world that is already changing around them. How people speak, listen, and respond in this environment shapes more than individual behavior. It influences how children learn to relate to others and to society. When conversation replaces withdrawal, when attention is chosen over distraction, and when flexibility is supported by clear structure, children may absorb these patterns as normal ways of moving through life.

What follows shares a set of observations. Each theme looks at how emotional development is taking shape. These sections are meant to encourage reflection, helping you notice what matches your own experience and how similar patterns may be appearing in the children around you. The purpose is to explore how emotional life may be changing and why those changes matter.

The Shape Of Family In A Changing World

Family has never followed a single pattern. Across history, it has shifted with economics, migration, belief systems, and social change. In some eras, it centered on survival and inheritance. In others, it emphasized duty and clearly defined roles. Today, it appears to revolve more openly around connection, belonging, and the everyday act of remaining involved in one another's lives.

Generation Alpha lives within what may be the broadest understanding of family to date. Homes may include one parent, two parents, grandparents, step siblings, co-parenting partnerships, or same-sex parents. Some family members live across town. Others live across oceans and connect through screens. The structure stretches. The language expands. Even so, the underlying function seems consistent. People gather in order to support one another through strain, transition, celebration, and ordinary days.

The design may be evolving, but the intention appears familiar. Children are still looking for reliability. Adults still attempt to create security. Across many forms, family continues to serve as the first environment where trust, conflict, forgiveness, and resilience are learned.

"Love has no blueprint. It only asks that we keep showing up." - *Santiago Dagon*

What is changing may not be the importance of family, but the recognition that it can take more than one shape. As those shapes multiply, the sense of belonging may be widening alongside them.

Home As Sanctuary

As culture moves faster each year, the idea of home is changing. It is no longer just a physical place. For many families, home is becoming a space shaped by intention. A place where the pace slows, expectations ease, and children can rest, make mistakes, laugh freely, or step back for a while and still feel safe and accepted.

Home may be one of the few places not governed by constant measurement. School tracks achievement. Social platforms reward visibility. Activities focus on skill. Within the household, many parents are trying to create something different. Not perfection, but safety. Not constant activity, but a place to recover and reset.

Some families are starting to protect unstructured time as carefully as earlier generations protected physical resources. A meal without devices. A walk with phones left in pockets. An evening shaped by conversation instead of scrolling. These moments are not dramatic. They are ordinary. They reflect a growing awareness that attention has become one of the most limited resources in modern life.

"Home is not where we are from. It is where the soul remembers to breathe." - *Santiago Dagon*

What may define the home as a sanctuary today is not separation from the world, but the ability to step away from its noise for a time. In that pause, essential learning continues to take shape.

Parenting In The Age Of Awareness

Parenting appears to be moving through a period of recalibration. In many households, authority is no longer expressed only through home rules and manners. It is increasingly expressed through dialogue. Structure remains important. Expectations still exist. Conversation now occupies more space within family life than it once did.

Children continue to need limits in order to feel secure. Clear boundaries often communicate care. At the same time, many parents are recognizing that listening carries its own form of influence. When a child feels heard, identity develops with less friction. Questions are explored rather than dismissed. Emotions are named rather than suppressed.

This New Humanity Shift does not remove tension, and at times it can create more of it. Finding balance is not simple. Too much control can weaken trust, while too much flexibility can create confusion. Most families move back and forth between these extremes, adjusting as needs and circumstances change.

Parenting, in this context, can be seen less as directing and more as accompanying. Parents become observers of emerging personalities while providing safety, values, and stability. The parenting role involves watching carefully. Intervening when necessary. Stepping back when growth requires space.

"To guide is not to control. It is to walk beside while the child finds their own direction." - *Santiago Dagon*

Perhaps what distinguishes this era is not that parents care more, but that awareness of emotional development has become more visible. And as that awareness grows, the relationship between parent and child may continue to evolve in ways that reflect both connection and change.

The New Language Of Love

Expressions of love appear to be evolving. In earlier generations, devotion was often measured through obligation and the need to put food on the table. Long hours of work. Material security. Sacrifice that was understood rather than discussed. Today, affection is increasingly recognized in smaller exchanges that happen throughout the day.

Attention has become something people feel and measure in daily interactions. It shows up in the tone of a reply, the timing of a response, and the choice to remain present rather than distracted. The decision to return to a conversation instead of withdrawing from it. These gestures may seem minor in isolation, but they accumulate in memory. Children often recall how they were treated in ordinary moments more clearly than what was said during major events.

In a culture saturated with distraction, focused attention holds meaning. When a parent looks up from a screen and listens fully, it signals value. When frustration is met with restraint instead of escalation, it signals safety. These patterns suggest that love is communicated less through grand declarations and more through consistency in everyday interaction.

"The purest form of love is attention." - *Santiago Dagon*

As attention becomes more deliberate, affection takes on a language that does not rely on dramatic display. It is built through repetition. Through clarity of mind. Through returning again and again to the relationship. Over time, that rhythm shapes how an Alpha child understands connection, trust, and worth.

The Grandparent Renaissance

Across many households, the role of grandparents appears to be expanding again. Longer life expectancy, digital communication, and changing family structures have drawn generations into closer contact, even when geography separates them. A grandparent may now attend a birthday through a screen or offer advice in a group message. Technology has shortened distance, but the influence of elders seems to rest on something older than connectivity.

Elders often carry a different tempo. Their memories were shaped in periods when information moved more slowly, and patience was built into daily life. Their stories are not delivered as updates. They unfold. And in that unfolding, children encounter another measure of time.

Generation Alpha is growing up in an environment defined by speed and access. Within that context, interaction with older relatives introduces contrast. A grandparent describing childhood without constant media, or recalling work done without digital tools, places current life in perspective. The comparison is rarely framed as better or worse. It simply reveals change.

These relationships can also offer emotional stability. Grandparents often give attention without the same pressures that shape parents. They observe more. They share stories. They connect everyday moments to a longer family narrative. In doing so, they help children see that identity extends beyond the present moment.

"The elder's task is not to be obeyed, but to be remembered." - *Santiago Dagon*

As the family structure evolves and expands, the reappearance of intergenerational dialogue suggests that wisdom is not replaced by innovation. It accumulates. And when children encounter stories that span decades, they begin to see their own lives as part of something still unfolding.

Siblings And The Social Laboratory

Within many homes, sibling relationships function as a small society. They offer companionship and competition, loyalty, and friction. Through brothers and sisters, children often encounter their first experiences of negotiation, boundary setting, alliance, and reconciliation. These exchanges can feel intense; however, they provide early rehearsal for life beyond the household.

Disagreement between siblings is rarely only about the immediate issue. It often reflects developing identity. One child asserts independence. Another tests influence. In the process, they learn that relationships can withstand tension. They discover that conflict does not automatically end connection.

For Generation Alpha, this dynamic extends beyond physical space. Siblings may collaborate in shared bedrooms or in digital environments where they build virtual worlds side by side. Even when separated by distance, they can create, compete, and communicate in real time. The shared experience, whether in a living room or on a platform, contributes to a sense of collective memory.

Many parents appear increasingly aware that comparison can erode this bond. Emphasizing difference without ranking it allows each child's strengths to develop without undermining another's. When individuality is acknowledged, sibling ties may feel less like rivalry and more like partnership.

"Siblings teach us that love can argue and still endure."
- Santiago Dagon

In these early social spaces, children begin to experience the complexity of closeness. They learn that care does not mean the absence of conflict, but the willingness to stay connected while working through it.

The Family As Emotional Classroom

Emotional understanding rarely begins with explanation. It develops through observation. Children watch how adults respond to inconvenience, disappointment, or surprise. They notice tone. They register facial expressions. They sense whether tension lingers or resolves.

In many ways, the household functions as an early classroom for emotional intelligence. A parent's patience during stress communicates more than a lecture about calm behavior. An apology offered after a difficult exchange demonstrates accountability in a way definitions cannot. Gratitude expressed at the end of a long day signals perspective.

Generation Alpha is growing up in a period when emotional vocabulary is more visible in schools and media. Words like emotional intelligence, empathy, and resilience appear in conversation more frequently than in past decades. What children see and experience at home continues to shape how they understand these ideas. Children often imitate what they observe long before they can articulate why.

The family environment also shows what happens after things go wrong. Misunderstandings occur. Voices rise. Fatigue shows. What happens next matters. When adults acknowledge mistakes and restore connection, children learn that relationships are not fragile things that must be protected from strain but living systems that can regain balance and continue.

"The child does not learn from what we say. They learn from how we live." - *Santiago Dagon*

Over time, these repeated patterns form an internal map. Self-awareness begins not as theory, but as recognition. And in that recognition, children start to understand both their own emotions and the emotions of others.

Dual Realities: The Physical And The Digital Home

For Generation Alpha, the boundary between physical and digital space is increasingly fluid. The bedroom may contain toys, books, and devices that connect instantly to classmates and friends. Conversations that begin at school continue online. Interests discovered through a screen often reappear at the kitchen table. The digital room is not separate from the household. It is woven into it.

This blending introduces complexity. Children move between environments with little hesitation. What adults sometimes view as divided attention may feel, to them, like a continuous social field. The question for families is less about exclusion and more about integration.

Many households are adjusting daily patterns to account for both realities. Meals set aside for conversation. Evenings structured around shared activity. Agreed boundaries that protect rest and in person interaction. These practices do not reject technology. They frame it. They suggest that devices are tools within a larger relational context.

Generation Alpha will likely grow up assuming this dual landscape as normal. What shapes their development is not the existence of digital space, but how it is modeled. When adults demonstrate balanced engagement, children observe how connection can extend through screens without replacing face to face exchange.

"Home is where silence can still be heard."

- Santiago Dagon

Within that space, whether physical or digital, the tone of interaction continues to matter. The signals that endure are not only technological. They are relational. And it is within that relationship that the meaning of home continues to form.

The Modern Village

The idea of the village has not disappeared. It has shifted form. Where support once came primarily from extended relatives and neighbors, it now includes teachers, coaches, mentors, counselors, online educators, and children's cable network shows whose influence enters the home. This is referred to as the Modern Village. Guidance can arrive from across town or across continents. Physical distance matters less than shared values and emotional understanding.

For many families, this expanded Modern Village influence offers opportunity. A child interested in music may learn from an instructor they have never met in person. A parent navigating uncertainty may find insight in a conversation hosted online. Community is no longer limited by geography. It is shaped by alignment and intention. YouTube, TikTok and many other streaming platforms are leading the way in forming the Modern Village where guidance is found and used.

At the same time, abundance introduces responsibility. Not every voice that attracts attention offers a healthy perspective. Volume in views, followers, or subscribers can be mistaken for credibility. Confidence can be disguised as expertise. Families are increasingly aware that discernment matters. The circles in the Modern Village that Alpha children form, whether local or digital, influence not only information but their tone, attitude, and worldview.

"A village is not where you live. It is where your soul feels accompanied." - *Santiago Dagon*

As this Modern Village continues to take shape, it reflects a broader cultural shift. Support systems are being reassembled in new ways. What remains constant is the need for belonging.

Within that need, families must continue to decide which voices help their children grow with clarity rather than confusion.

The Future Of Family Values

Family values have never remained fixed. They tend to reflect the pressures and possibilities of their time. In earlier generations, obedience, and conformity often signaled stability. Clear parental hierarchies of authority offered predictability in uncertain conditions. Today, the emphasis in many households appears to be shifting toward openness and mutual understanding.

Conversations that were once avoided are now more visible. Mental health, identity, bullying, emotional strain, and social change enter family dialogue with greater frequency. This does not mean agreement is automatic. It suggests that silence is no longer the default response to complexity.

Strength within the family system is also being reconsidered. It is less associated with rigidity and more with adaptability. A household that can adjust to new information, changing circumstances, or evolving identities often maintains cohesion more effectively than one that resists every shift. Flexibility, in this sense, does not signal weakness. It signals responsiveness.

Respect, too, is being reframed. It moves in more than one direction. Children observe how adults speak to one another. Adults observe how children internalize those interactions. Authority remains present, and it is increasingly linked to consistency rather than control.

"Respect is not demanded. It is demonstrated."

- Santiago Dagon

As cultural conditions continue to change, family values are likely to keep adapting. What endures is not a single rule set, but the intention to create environments where truth can be expressed and relationships can withstand honesty.

The Circle Of Care

No family exists in isolation. Even the most private households participate in a broader network of neighbors, schools, workplaces, and shared environments. What is practiced within the home often moves outward, shaping how individuals engage with the wider community.

Children notice how adults treat friends and coworkers, how they respond to disagreement, and how they gossip about people who are not present. These behaviors form an early template for how children engage with the wider world. Compassion practiced at home does not stay there. It becomes a reference point. Patience shown during a difficult conversation can later shape how a child handles conflict with peers. Forgiveness exchanged at the dinner table may influence how disagreements are handled beyond the front door.

Generation Alpha is growing up in a time when global events are immediately present. News, climate concerns, social movements, and cultural debates enter the home in real time. How families talk about and make sense of these events shapes how children come to understand responsibility beyond themselves.

Care, in this sense, functions as a circle. It begins in daily interaction and gradually widens. The tone established in close relationships often echoes in public life.

"The love we practice in private becomes the peace we offer in public." - *Santiago Dagon*

As families consider their role in a changing society, the connection between home and world becomes more visible. The habits formed in personal spaces may influence how the next generation participates in collective life.

Closing Reflection

The family can be understood as an ecosystem in its earliest form. And now the Modern Village. It is the setting where trust begins to take root and where missteps are absorbed into learning rather than recorded as failure. Growth rarely happens in a straight line. It unfolds through repetition, repair, and shared experience. Within the household, those cycles are lived daily.

Technology may continue to speed up daily routines and widen access to information. Schedules may grow tighter, and demands may increase. Even so, the quality of relationships inside the home remains fundamental. Children tend to remember less about how efficiently a household functioned and more about how it felt to live there.

Generation Alpha will inherit opportunities that cross borders and disciplines, along with tools earlier generations could not have imagined. Even so, their earliest sense of security is likely to form at home through simple experiences: being heard, being acknowledged, and being accompanied through difficulty.

"The future will not be built by technology or ideas alone. It will be built by families who remember how to care."
- Santiago Dagon

When empathy is practiced in conversation, when forgiveness follows conflict, when shared laughter returns after strain, something enduring is formed. Progress may reshape society. Belonging shapes the person who moves within it.

PART III

THE OUTER HORIZON

CHAPTER 11

THE GLOBAL VILLAGE

"The world no longer turns on geography. It turns on understanding." - *Santiago Dagon*

Generation Alpha is growing up in a world that feels both vast and immediate. The Modern Village, the family ecosystem, unfolds across continents into the Global Village. It arrives in the palm of a hand within seconds. Languages translate in real time. Cultural expressions travel without passports. The idea of distance has not disappeared. Distance no longer defines the limits of awareness.

For much of history, community was shaped primarily by geography. Identity formed within neighborhoods, faith traditions, and local customs. Information moved slowly enough to be absorbed before the next wave arrived. Today, children encounter a constant streaming of perspectives, images, and conversations that extend far beyond their immediate surroundings.

This expansion does not replace local belonging. It layers over it. A child may feel rooted in family and school while also participating in digital spaces that span countries and cultures. Exposure to diversity becomes ordinary rather than exceptional. Difference is not something discovered later in life. It is present from the beginning.

Such visibility carries both opportunity and complexity. Empathy can widen. Curiosity can deepen. At the same time, the sheer volume of voices can challenge attention and discernment. The Global Village invites connection. It also asks for emotional resilience.

The themes explored in this chapter consider how this extended environment may influence identity, responsibility, communication, and belonging. The focus is not on technology alone. It is on how human development unfolds within an interconnected landscape.

Each theme offers a glimpse into how emotional development might unfold within a culture shaped by continual connection and rapid change. Notice what aligns with your own experiences. The intention is not to predict. It is to examine how emotional life may be shifting in the decades ahead.

The Village Expands

For much of history, daily life unfolded within visible boundaries. Geography shaped opportunity. Custom shaped identity. A village defined not only where someone lived, but what they were likely to become. Stories were passed down within walking distance. Imagination was often limited by proximity.

That context has widened. The digital environment now functions as an additional neighborhood, and perhaps a home or family to some Generation Alpha children, layered over their physical space. A child can speak with someone across the world as easily as with a classmate down the street. Cultural references, music, humor, and ideas move across borders with little resistance. What once required travel now requires connection.

Generation Alpha is growing up inside this expanded landscape. Friendships may form through shared interests rather than shared streets. A conversation that begins in one country can continue in another without pause. Laughter, collaboration, and curiosity travel quickly. Physical distance remains real; however, it no longer defines the limits of interaction in the same way.

This New Humanity Shift carries both opportunity and complexity. Exposure to diverse experiences can broaden understanding. It can also introduce competing narratives at an early age. Children are encountering perspectives that previous generations might not have seen until adulthood.

"Every signal we send into the world is a whisper in the shared dream of humanity." - *Santiago Dagon*

As the village expands, belonging appears less tied to location and more connected to shared values. Generation Alpha is learning to navigate a geography shaped by land. It is also shaped by networks. Within that landscape, the idea of community continues to evolve.

The New Geography Of Belonging

Belonging once drew its strength from location. Accent, neighborhood, religious tradition, and landscape shaped identity in visible ways. A person's sense of place was often inherited rather than chosen. Community formed around shared proximity and long-standing custom.

That framework is shifting. Belonging now appears increasingly connected to recognition rather than geography. The defining question is less about where someone lives and more about where they feel seen. Digital platforms allow individuals to gather around interests, values, and experiences that may not exist within their immediate surroundings.

Generation Alpha exists within multiple overlapping circles. Some are rooted in family and local culture. Others are formed through shared passions that stretch across continents. A child may identify with classmates, an online creative community, a cultural heritage group, and a global cause all at once. These affiliations can coexist without canceling one another.

This widened field introduces freedom; however,

it can also create ambiguity. When connection is abundant, stability may require intention. Exposure to many perspectives can enrich identity, while also raising questions about where one fully fits. The experience of belonging becomes layered rather than singular.

"We belong not where we are born, but where we are understood." - *Santiago Dagon*

As this geography continues to evolve, belonging seems less tied to coordinates and more linked to connection. Recognition, empathy, and shared values may shape identity as strongly as location once did. In the New Humanity Shift, the idea of home and the need to belong extends beyond land into digital intimacy. Digital intimacy refers to the sense of emotional closeness, trust, and connection that develops through digital platforms such as messaging, social media, and video calls.

Language Without Borders

For much of history, language marked clear boundaries. Dialects signaled origin. Accents revealed region. Translation required time, and misunderstanding often limited exchange. Communication moved at the pace of human travel and shared space.

Today, translation appears almost instantly. A message written in one language can be read in another within seconds. Children encounter words, phrases, and expressions from cultures far beyond their immediate environment. They may hear multiple languages in a single day, often without noticing the shift.

This accessibility expands possibilities. It allows collaboration and friendship across distance. It introduces ideas that might otherwise remain unfamiliar. Speed can also compress understanding. When communication becomes effortless, layers of tone, context, and cultural history can thin. Humor does not always travel intact. Emotion may lose its depth when condensed into brief exchanges.

"When words become effortless, we must work harder to listen." - *Santiago Dagon*

Generation Alpha is developing a communication style shaped by symbols, abbreviations, images, and shared references. On the surface, vocabulary may appear reduced. Beneath it, emotional signaling can be complex. A single icon may carry layers of meaning understood within a particular group.

As language continues to cross borders with ease, listening may require greater attention. Understanding may depend less on fluency alone and more on sensitivity to context. In this expanding field of expression, connection will not rely on words alone. It will depend on the intention carried within them.

Culture In Motion

Culture once moved at the pace of migration and trade. It was shaped by geography, preserved through tradition, and passed down within defined communities. Change occurred, but gradually. Influence traveled in visible waves.

Today, culture circulates continuously. Music, fashion, humor, food, and artistic expression cross borders within hours. An Alpha child's playlist may blend artists from several continents. A recipe may combine techniques rooted in different histories. Slang can originate in one city and appear globally before the weekend.

This movement creates texture and variety. It also introduces tension. When cultural elements circulate widely, questions of origin and ownership become more complex. Some find comfort in clearly defined heritage. Others embrace hybrid expressions as a reflection of lived reality.

Generation Alpha is growing up in this state of motion. They encounter influence from multiple traditions at once. Identity may be formed less by singular lineage and more by layered experience. Exposure to diversity becomes routine rather than exceptional.

"Culture is not a museum. It is a conversation that never ends." - *Santiago Dagon*

In this ongoing exchange, authenticity may be less about preserving an unchanged form and more about acknowledging roots while participating in evolution. As culture continues to move, uniformity does not endure. Continuity of purpose carries forward through new expressions.

The Rise Of Global Empathy

Digital networks connect information with remarkable speed. Alongside that exchange, emotional exposure has expanded. Children today can witness celebrations, crises, injustice, and resilience from nearly any region in real time. Events that once remained distant now enter daily awareness.

Generation Alpha is immersed with this immediacy. They may see images of natural disasters, social movements, and cultural milestones long before they fully understand their complexity. Exposure can broaden perspective. It can also create emotional strain. When the world feels constantly visible, the responsibility to care may feel expansive.

Empathy in this context becomes both opportunity and challenge. The ability to recognize another person's experience across distance can deepen understanding. At the same time, constant awareness can blur boundaries between what is personal and what is global.

"When the heart becomes global, the world begins to heal."
- Santiago Dagon

How Generation Alpha integrates such awareness is too early to determine. Perhaps, some could channel concern into focused action within their immediate communities. Others could seek ways to participate in larger conversations. Global empathy does not require solving every issue at once. It often begins with sustained attention to one place, one person, and one cause.

As emotional visibility continues to expand, the capacity to balance concern with resilience may shape how empathy matures in the years ahead.

Digital Citizenship And The Ethics Of Connection

As community expands beyond geography, responsibility expands with it. Communication no longer occurs only within familiar circles. A comment can travel beyond its intended audience. A brief message can be amplified, interpreted, and reshaped in ways the sender did not anticipate.

For Generation Alpha, the digital environment is not separate from daily life. It is intertwined with friendships, learning, and identity. Interactions that occur through screens often carry emotional impact equal to those that happen face to face. The distinction between "online" and "real" continues to blur.

This reality introduces ethical questions at an earlier age. Tone, timing, and intention matter. Humor can misfire. Criticism can escalate. Silence can signal indifference. Children observe how adults navigate disagreement and expression in public spaces. They notice whether accountability follows harm or whether volume replaces reflection.

"Freedom online is no different from freedom anywhere else. It ends where harm begins." - *Santiago Dagon*

Digital citizenship appears less about technical skill and more about relational awareness. Courtesy, empathy, and restraint influence not only personal reputation, but collective atmosphere. As this generation matures within a connected world, their understanding of consequence may shape how these networks evolve.

Connection offers reach. The question that remains unfolding is how that reach will be guided.

Collaboration Across Continents

Cooperation is no longer limited by shared location. Increasingly, projects unfold across time zones. A student in one country can contribute to a design started in another. A science experiment can be refined through shared data collected on different continents. Creative work, once shaped within local circles, now develops through distributed teams.

Generation Alpha is entering a landscape where collaboration across distance may feel routine. Digital platforms allow children to exchange ideas, revise one another's work, and solve problems collectively. The experience of building something with people whose languages, customs, and daily realities differ can broaden perspective in ways textbooks alone cannot.

This New Humanity Shift also changes how achievement is understood. Recognition may move from individual performance toward shared contribution. Success becomes less about standing apart and more about participating effectively. Negotiation, patience, and cross-cultural awareness gain importance alongside technical skill.

"When we create together, the planet becomes our classroom." - Santiago Dagon

As collective projects become more common, intelligence may be expressed through coordination rather than competition. Knowledge does not diminish when shared. It multiplies. In that exchange, learning becomes less isolated and more interconnected, reflecting the structure of the world in which this generation is growing.

The New Tribalism

Greater connection has not eliminated the human desire for smaller circles. If anything, it has intensified it. Within vast networks, people often gather into focused communities organized around shared interests, beliefs, humor, or identity. These digital groupings can offer companionship and affirmation, especially for those who may feel isolated in their immediate surroundings.

For Generation Alpha, participation in multiple circles may feel natural. A child might belong to a local sports team, an online gaming community, a cultural heritage group, and a global interest forum at the same time. Each circle provides language, norms, and shared references.

However, strong affiliation can narrow perspective if not balanced with exposure. Agreement may begin to resemble certainty. Repetition can reinforce assumptions of both truth and false narratives. When communities become insulated, curiosity may give way to defensiveness.

"To meet another's truth without fear is the beginning of wisdom." - *Santiago Dagon*

The ability to engage across differences may become increasingly significant. Listening without immediate dismissal. Asking questions before reacting. Holding conviction without hostility. In a connected world composed of many intersecting circles, diversity does not disappear. It becomes more visible. How this generation learns to navigate that visibility may influence whether connection leads to fragmentation or deeper understanding.

Migration Of Hearts And Homes

Movement has always shaped human history. Its pace and visibility have intensified in the present era. Families relocate for safety, education, employment, relationship, or exploration.

Children may grow up in one country while maintaining ties to another. They may speak one language at school and another at home. Identity becomes layered through lived experience rather than confined to a single setting.

For Generation Alpha, cultural fluidity may feel ordinary. A child might celebrate traditions from multiple regions, navigate differing social norms, and shift comfortably between contexts. This mobility can expand perspective. It can also introduce complexity as they reconcile expectations that do not always align.

"Home is the story we keep rewriting wherever we arrive."
- Santiago Dagon

Belonging in this landscape appears less fixed and more adaptive. Identity may resemble a collage assembled over time, shaped by memory, language, and relationship. Translation extends beyond vocabulary. It includes tone, gesture, and emotional reference points that vary across cultures.

What may seem fragmented from a distance often becomes integrative from within. Generation Alpha children who move easily between different environments often develop a strong awareness of slight differences. They learn to read context carefully. They become aware of how meaning shifts depending on setting.

As migration continues to influence families, the definition of home broadens. It becomes less about singular origin and more about the continuity of care carried from place to place. In that continuity, identity is not reduced. It is expanded.

The Planet As Family

The idea of belonging appears to be extending beyond human circles. Environmental awareness now enters childhood through school lessons, media, and daily conversation. Forest fires, rising seas, endangered species, and shifting climates are not distant abstractions. They are part of the atmosphere in which Generation Alpha is growing up in.

For many children, nature is not framed only as scenery. It is discussed as interdependence. Food systems, water cycles, and energy use are explained as connected processes rather than isolated topics. The language of stewardship is increasingly present in both classrooms and households.

"We are not guests on Earth. We are its memory and its promise." - *Santiago Dagon*

This perspective suggests a relational New Humanity Shift. The natural world is seen less as resource alone and more as shared inheritance. Concern for environmental balance is woven into a child's identity formation, not positioned as a separate cause reserved for adulthood.

Generation Alpha is likely to approach planetary care as part of ordinary responsibility. Recycling, conservation, and sustainable choices may feel habitual rather than exceptional. The broader implication is cultural. When the planet is understood as interconnected with daily life, decisions take on broader significance.

How this awareness matures will depend on guidance, opportunity, and lived examples. What is visible now is a widening frame of reference. The circle of care continues to grow, including landscapes and ecosystems within the language of belonging.

The Rhythm Of Unity

Unity is often imagined as sameness. In practice, it appears closer to understanding. It does not erase difference. It creates space for difference to exist without immediate conflict. Within a connected world, exposure to contrasting beliefs, customs, and experiences is routine. The question is not whether diversity will appear, but how it will be received.

Generation Alpha lives within a world marked by visible variation. Cultural expressions, political viewpoints, and personal identity are shared openly and widely. Encountering differences may feel less unusual than in previous decades. What remains complex is interpretation. Listening across disagreement requires restraint. It asks for curiosity before reaction.

"Unity is not one melody sung by all. It is harmony between many notes." - *Santiago Dagon*

Harmony does not imply uniformity. It suggests coordination within variety. In a global context, unity may depend less on shared opinion and more on shared recognition of dignity. The desire to connect appears persistent, even when conversation becomes strained.

The world continues to produce noise. Information competes for attention. Strong opinions circulate quickly. Beneath that surface activity, the impulse toward relationship remains visible. How Generation Alpha engages that impulse may influence whether connection becomes deeper or more fragmented in the years ahead. Generation Alpha may turn that desire into something lasting.

Closing Reflection

The Global Village does not exist only in infrastructure or technology. It forms within perception. It expands when individuals recognize connection beyond proximity and see shared humanity beneath differences. Borders may still define nations. Belonging increasingly extends across them through relationship and exchange.

As networks widen, the internal posture toward others becomes significant. Curiosity can replace suspicion. Awareness can temper reaction. When understanding grows, distance loses some of its power to divide.

"The borders of the future are drawn in the heart."

- Santiago Dagon

Generation Alpha is inheriting systems of connection that operate continuously. How they engage those systems will shape their sense of purpose and direction. If empathy guides communication, conversations are more likely to lead to understanding rather than division. If humility accompanies achievement, collaboration strengthens. And, if care guides interactions, technology remains a tool rather than a replacement for genuine connection.

The visible network is made of devices and signals. The enduring network is built through attention, accountability, and mutual respect. In that recognition, the idea of a Global Village moves from metaphor to lived experience.

CHAPTER 12

TECHNOLOGY AS A PARTNER

"Every tool we build is a mirror. The question is never how smart it becomes, but how clearly we can still see ourselves within it." - *Santiago Dagon*

Technology is no longer something children simply use. It is something they grow alongside. Devices respond, adapt, and participate in daily routines from early childhood. Questions are answered instantly. Images are generated in seconds. Conversations unfold with systems designed to anticipate response. For Generation Alpha, this environment feels less like novelty and more like atmosphere.

In earlier eras, tools extended physical strength or simplified labor. Today's technologies increasingly interact with cognition and emotion. They assist with homework, suggest creative directions, track health patterns, and simulate dialogue. The relationship is shifting from operation to interaction. The New Humanity Shift invites new reflections about influence, intention, and identity.

Partnership implies reciprocity, even when one side is not human. Digital systems refine themselves based on engagement. They respond to habits, amplify preferences, and mirror behavior. In that exchange, Generation Alpha children are not passive recipients. They are participants shaping the systems that shape them.

This chapter explores how such digital partnerships may influence creativity, ethics, education, intimacy, work, and environmental awareness. The focus is not on fear or celebration, but on awareness. Technology neither guarantees progress nor ensures decline. Its impact depends on how it is guided, interpreted, and integrated into human development.

The reflections that follow are not definitive answers. They are considered observations and thematic explorations. Each section looks at how emotional growth and moral awareness may evolve within a landscape where intelligence is increasingly shared between human and machine.

You are invited to engage these pages as thoughtful inquiry rather than final judgment. Notice what resonates with your own experience. Observe how these dynamics appear in the young people you encounter. The aim is not to forecast a fixed outcome. It is to explore how the inner life of a generation may be adapting within a rapidly transforming world.

Beyond The Fear Of Machines

New inventions rarely arrive without tension. Fire altered survival. Industrial engines reshaped labor. Early computers introduced unfamiliar forms of thinking. Each advance prompted questions about what might be gained and what might be diminished.

Artificial intelligence now occupies a similar space in public conversation. It inspires fascination and concern in equal measures. Some view it as amplification of human capability. Others see risk in its speed and autonomy. Beneath both responses lies a deeper question about identity. When machines perform tasks once reserved for people, what remains distinctly human?

History suggests that technology does not erase the human element. It reveals priorities. Tools tend to magnify intention. When guided with care, they extend creativity and efficiency. When used without reflection, they can intensify distraction or imbalance. The outcome often depends less on the tool itself and more on the values surrounding its use.

"We are not competing with our creations. We are completing them." - *Santiago Dagon*

Generation Alpha will grow up alongside systems that compose text, generate images, analyze data, and simulate conversation. For them, these capabilities may feel ordinary. The distinction between human effort and machine assistance will require thoughtful navigation.

What appears to endure across ages is the role of judgment, empathy, and sense-making. A system may produce answers. Discernment remains human. A program may generate content. Interpretation belongs to the person receiving it.

As technology becomes more capable, the question shifts from performance to purpose. In that shift, humanity is not diminished. It becomes clarified.

The End Of Tool, The Beginning Of Partnership

For much of history, tools responded only when directed. A hammer required force. A wheel required motion. A pen required a guiding hand. Action began and ended with the user. The relationship between person and object was clear.

That distinction is becoming less defined. Contemporary technologies respond, adapt, and in some cases anticipate. Devices suggest next steps. Systems refine themselves through use. Interaction can feel conversational rather than mechanical. The experience shifts from operating a tool to engaging with a responsive system.

This evolution introduces a different kind of responsibility. When technology appears to "understand," the human role can seem less visible. Awareness remains central. Intelligent systems may increase efficiency. They do not determine purpose. They can assist with research, design, and organization. They cannot decide what is worth pursuing.

"When we give a tool a voice, we must also give ourselves silence enough to hear our own." - *Santiago Dagon*

Generation Alpha is likely to approach these digital partnerships as routine. Collaboration with digital systems may feel natural. The distinction they will navigate is not whether to use technology. It is how to remain reflective while doing so.

Cooperation does not require surrender. It requires clarity. When curiosity and conscience remain active, tools extend capacity without replacing direction. In that balance, digital partnership becomes less about dependence and more about intentional use.

The New Co Creativity

Creativity has long been associated with individual originality. An artist alone with a canvas. A writer facing a blank page. A composer experimenting at a piano. The image of creation often centered on solitude and personal expression.

That image is changing. Digital systems now assist with drafting, editing, visual design, and musical composition. A child might outline a story and use a program to expand its setting. A melody may begin in a bedroom and be refined with algorithmic suggestions. The act of making becomes collaborative, even when one partner is nonhuman.

This development raises questions about authorship and influence. When technology contributes structure or variation, where does creativity reside? The answer may depend on intention. Machines can generate patterns based on data. They can combine elements in new configurations. What they do not possess is lived experiences. They do not attach memory, emotion, or personal meaning to what is produced.

"Creation has never been about ownership. It is about participation in the unfolding of possibility."

- Santiago Dagon

Generation Alpha will likely approach co-creation as natural. They may not separate human imagination from digital enhancement in rigid ways. Instead, they may move between them fluidly. The guiding force remains internal. A system can suggest. A person decides what resonates.

Human creativity continues to shape direction. Purpose arises not only from what is made, but from why it is made. In that distinction, collaboration expands possibility while the core impulse to express remains distinctly human.

The Ethics Of Intelligence

As digital systems assume greater roles in decision making, the conversation shifts from capability to consequence. Algorithms now influence access to information, financial opportunities, medical recommendations, and public visibility. Their reach extends gradually into areas that shape daily life.

These systems are not neutral in the abstract. They reflect the data, assumptions, and priorities embedded within them. When patterns of bias exist in society, they can surface in code. When efficiency is valued above equity, outcomes may reflect that emphasis. The question becomes not only what technology can do. It also becomes what it ought to do.

"A mind without empathy is powerful but blind."

- Santiago Dagon

Generation Alpha will grow up aware that intelligence is not limited to humans. They will interact with systems that simulate reasoning and prediction. Simulation does not equal conscience. Ethical direction still originates with people.

Developing this awareness requires more than technical skill. It involves understanding impact, context, and responsibility. Before shaping the tools of the future, young people will need to recognize how values inform design. Empathy, fairness, and accountability are not features that emerge automatically. They are cultivated.

As intelligence becomes distributed across networks and platforms, the human element remains central. Technology may execute. Judgment continues to guide. The balance between innovation and integrity will depend on how carefully these principles are held.

Digital Intimacy

Technology is moving beyond information exchange into emotional interaction. Devices can detect tone shifts, track facial expression, and respond with programmed reassurance. Digital companions simulate conversation, offer reminders to pause, and provide structured support during moments of stress. For some, these interactions feel accessible and immediate.

This development raises new questions about attachment and perception. When a system responds with empathy coded into its design, the experience may resemble companionship. However, resemblance is different from shared experience. A programmed reply can acknowledge distress. It does not carry lived vulnerability.

"A machine can mirror your voice. Only another heart can echo your silence." - *Santiago Dagon*

Generation Alpha will grow up navigating these distinctions. Emotional support delivered through technology can be helpful when people feel disconnected. It can help organize thoughts, suggest coping strategies, or offer a sense of ongoing conversation. At the same time, deeper connection usually develops through shared experiences, mutual involvement, and the unpredictability of real interaction.

For Generation Alpha, learning to tell the difference between simulated interaction and real mutual connection may become an important part of their emotional development. Digital comfort and support can be helpful, especially in guiding or calming moments. Still, what shapes identity most deeply is the experience of being truly known by another person who brings their own thoughts, feelings, and inner world into the relationship.

As digital systems become more responsive, clarity around human relationship may grow more significant rather than less.

Technology In Education And Healing

Digital systems are increasingly present in classrooms and therapeutic settings. Adaptive learning platforms can adjust to a student's pace, revisit concepts without frustration, and provide immediate feedback. Virtual simulations will allow Generation Alpha children to explore environments that would otherwise remain inaccessible. In clinical contexts, immersive tools are being used to help individuals revisit memories, practice coping strategies, or rehearse difficult conversations.

These developments expand access. A child who struggles in a traditional classroom may find help in a personalized format. A patient hesitant to speak aloud may begin with guided interaction through a screen. Technology can extend reach where resources are limited and offer consistency where human time is constrained.

"Innovation without compassion is just acceleration."

- Santiago Dagon

For Generation Alpha, learning and healing involve more than information or technique. They rely on real relationships. Encouragement carries tone and timing. Trust grows through repeated, shared experiences. A digital tutor can adjust difficulty levels, but a classroom teacher notices posture, mood, and attention. An app can guide breathing or calming exercises. A counselor, coach, or parent can sense hesitation, confusion, or stress behind a child's words.

What remains essential is human engagement. Compassion cannot be automated. It is expressed through attention, responsiveness, and accountability. As education and medicine integrate advanced systems, the quality of connection may continue to determine depth of impact.

Environmental Technology And The Reconnection With Earth

Industrial progress once focused on extraction and expansion. Forests were cleared to fuel growth. Rivers were redirected in the name of efficiency. Innovation often valued output more than balance. In recent decades, this direction has begun to change. Technology is increasingly being used to produce more. It is also being applied to restore what has been strained or damaged.

New systems monitor air quality, track wildlife migration, and map ocean temperatures in real time. Reforestation efforts now use drones to plant trees at large scale. Data platforms help communities measure consumption and adjust behavior. What was once invisible becomes measurable. What was once distant becomes visible.

"The planet does not need saving. It needs remembering."
- Santiago Dagon

For Generation Alpha, environmental awareness is closely linked to technological literacy. The same tools they use for entertainment and communication can also show patterns of climate change and stress on ecosystems. How those tools are used makes the difference. Technology can speed up depletion, or it can support recovery.

This generation is likely to experience environmental systems as connected rather than separate. Sensors, satellites, and predictive models can reveal patterns and risks. Information alone does not shape outcomes. How these tools are used still depends on human choice. As technology becomes more powerful, the link between innovation and responsibility becomes harder to ignore. Monitoring requires follow-through. Care requires intention. The central question is no longer whether technology can affect the planet, but how thoughtfully it will be directed.

Work And The Human Purpose

Automation is altering the structure of labor. Tasks that once required sustained human effort are increasingly handled by systems capable of repetition, calculation, and optimization. Entire industries are adjusting. The shift is not only technical. It is cultural.

For generations, work was closely tied to survival and stability. Identity often formed around occupation. The question "What do you do?" carried significance beyond income. As automation reduces reliance on certain forms of manual or routine labor, the definition of contribution may continue to evolve.

"When labor is freed from necessity, purpose must take its place." - *Santiago Dagon*

Generation Alpha may encounter a landscape where productivity is no longer the sole measure of value. Creativity, collaboration, and service could hold greater emphasis as repetitive processes become automated. Work may increasingly involve interpretation, design, relationship, and problem solving that extends beyond mechanical execution.

This transition also introduces uncertainty. If machines handle efficiency, individuals may reconsider how they define purpose. Fulfillment may not automatically replace obligation. It may require reflection and adaptation.

As economic systems adjust, the connection between labor and identity will likely remain central. What may shift is emphasis. Contribution could become less about output alone and more about impact, relevance, and human engagement. In that recalibration, work becomes less about endurance and more about alignment with purpose.

The Digital Soul

Much of human memory now resides in digital form. Photographs are stored in clouds rather than albums. Messages remain searchable years after they are written. Voices can be replayed long after a conversation ends. Personal history is increasingly archived in code.

The New Humanity Shift changes how remembrance is experienced. Earlier generations relied on physical objects to preserve stories. Letters faded. Film deteriorated. Memory required retelling. Today, preservation feels automatic. Moments are captured and retained with little effort. The digital record expands continuously.

"Eternity is not how long we are remembered, but how deeply we have lived." - *Santiago Dagon*

For Generation Alpha, the concept of legacy may look different from that of their grandparents. Material inheritance may hold less symbolic meaning than the traces left in shared platforms, collaborative projects, or recorded exchanges. The archive will be extensive. What remains uncertain is how it will be interpreted.

Technology can preserve data. It cannot assign depth. A stored image does not convey the full context of the moment it represents. A saved message does not capture the emotional landscape surrounding it. Understanding continues to arise from lived experience rather than storage capacity.

As digital memory expands, the distinction between record and reality may grow more important. The archive may endure. The significance of what it contains will still depend on how fully it was lived.

Technology As Reflection, Not Replacement

Each major invention has extended a human capacity. The telescope widened sight. The printing press multiplied ideas. The microphone amplified voice. Tools have often functioned as mirrors as much as instruments. They reveal how we think, what we prioritize, and where we direct attention.

Artificial intelligence continues this pattern. It does more than automate tasks. It reflects patterns embedded within human behavior. It highlights preferences, assumptions, and habits that might otherwise remain unnoticed. When systems produce biased outcomes, they often mirror the bias present in the data that shaped them. When they streamline communication, they reveal how frequently we seek efficiency over depth.

"The purpose of progress is not control. It is consciousness."

- Santiago Dagon

For Generation Alpha, technology may feel inseparable from daily life. The distinction between user and system may blur in gradual ways. But the reflective function remains. Tools can illuminate blind spots. They can prompt questions about intention and impact.

Technology does not replace human judgment. It strengthens the values that guide how it is used. When guided by care, it can expand awareness and creativity. When used without reflection, it can increase distraction or cause harm. In this way, innovation becomes less about controlling the environment and more about examining ourselves.

As tools become more powerful, the task is not to step away from them. It is to understand what they reveal about the people who create and use them.

Toward A Conscious Partnership

Digital partnership requires awareness. It assumes interaction is active and shaped by choice, not something that simply happens to us. Digital systems respond to input and adjust based on how they are used. Over time, they are shaped by the habits and values of the people who engage with them.

Machines do not have awareness of their own. They reflect accumulated behavior. Search histories influence recommendations. Engagement patterns affect what becomes visible. Gradually, systems begin to mirror collective preference. Careful use leads in one direction. Careless use leads in another.

"The highest intelligence is not invention, but intention."
- Santiago Dagon

Generation Alpha will grow up using technologies that change based on how people use them. As these children become students, creators, and later the ones who design and choose these tools, the role of intention becomes clearer. Learning technology can be built to help students work together, or it can be built to measure, rank, and compare them constantly. Classroom platforms can support careful thinking and respectful discussion, or they can encourage fast reactions and disagreement. The choices made in designing and using these systems will directly shape how children experience learning every day.

The direction of technology will not be set by capability alone. It will also reflect the values built into design and reinforced through daily use. When intention prioritizes connection, systems can support relationships. When focus rests only on attention and growth metrics, other human qualities tend to fade.

A conscious partnership with technology does not reject innovation. It places it within ethical awareness. As Generation Alpha helps shape the next wave of tools, the tone they establish may influence not just how technology works, but how culture itself unfolds.

Closing Reflection

Technology does not determine the future on its own. It functions more like a surface upon which choices are expressed. Systems retain patterns, reflect behavior, and extend intention. In that sense, they carry traces of the values that shaped them.

Digital memory accumulates gradually. Preferences, priorities, and habits become embedded in design and data. The tools that surround daily life are influenced not only by engineering. They are also shaped by the culture that directs their development. What is emphasized becomes amplified.

"We are not building the future. We are teaching the future how to feel." - *Santiago Dagon*

Generation Alpha will grow alongside systems that operate with increasing speed and precision. What may matter most is not what these systems can do, but how they are oriented. Intelligence can exist alongside empathy. Efficiency can leave room for reflection. Innovation can stay connected to human connection.

When technology is guided by awareness, it does not replace meaning. It extends it. Progress then becomes less about moving faster and more about staying aligned with values that support connection. In that alignment, advancement serves life instead of overwhelming it.

CHAPTER 13

WORK, PURPOSE, AND THE
REDEFINITION OF SUCCESS

"Success is not reaching the top. It is remembering what you were climbing for." - *Santiago Dagon*

Few forces shape identity as strongly as work. For generations, a person's occupation has signaled status, stability, and belonging. It has organized daily life, shaped relationships, and marked the transition into adulthood. In many societies, success followed a familiar path: education, steady advancement, accumulation, and retirement. Generation Alpha is entering the world as this model of work and success is being reshaped.

Automation is altering industries. Remote systems are dissolving geographic limits. Careers no longer unfold in predictable lines. At the same time, conversations about burnout, alignment, well-being, and ethical enterprises are becoming more visible. Generation Alpha children are watching adults and their parents question long-held assumptions about productivity and worth.

Work is increasingly described not only as a way to earn a living, but as a form of expression. Ideas like purpose are now part of conversations that once focused only on ambition. Success is being measured not just by external approval. It is also measured by a sense of inner consistency. These changes do not remove financial realities. They widen how people think and talk about them.

As structures evolve, young people will inherit both opportunity and ambiguity. Choice will widen. Direction will require discernment. The question may no longer be simply "How far can I go?" but "Who am I becoming as I move?"

The sections that follow are not definitive claims about what will happen next. They are considered reflections on patterns already visible. Each theme explores how identity, resilience, and aspiration may develop within an era where connectivity accelerates change and stability is increasingly self-defined.

You are invited to approach these pages as thoughtful inquiry rather than instruction. Notice where your own observations intersect. Consider how these themes surface in the lives of the children you know. The aim is not to forecast a single outcome. This section examines how people may begin to see work and success differently in the New Humanity Shift.

The End Of The Career Ladder

For much of the twentieth century, work often followed a recognizable arc. Education prepared a person for a defined field. Employment began near the base of an organization. Advancement came gradually through loyalty and tenure. The structure resembled a ladder: linear, upward, and relatively predictable.

That framework is becoming less common. Industries evolve quickly. Roles appear and disappear within a decade. Skills that once lasted a lifetime now require renewal. Instead of a single vertical path, many careers unfold laterally, diagonally, or in cycles. The image of a web may better describe the landscape than a staircase.

For Generation Alpha, this sense of flexibility is becoming a baseline expectation. They see adults change professions, build multiple income streams, and combine creative and technical skills. As a result, the idea of staying in one role or institution for life may feel less important than the ability to adapt and evolve.

The New Humanity Shift introduces both possibility and ambiguity. Without a clearly marked path, direction requires reflection. The absence of rigid structure can invite experimentation. It can also create uncertainty. Movement becomes intentional rather than automatic.

"The world no longer rewards endurance of the wrong path. It rewards awareness of the right one."

- Santiago Dagon

Success within this environment may depend less on persistence alone and more on alignment. Stability may emerge not from staying in one place, but from understanding what remains important across change. As the architecture of work evolves, identity may be shaped less by position and more by coherence between values and action.

The Purpose Of Work

Work has long served practical needs. It provided food, shelter, and security. At the same time, it offered something less tangible. Through labor, individuals signaled participation in a shared world. Occupation became a way of answering the question, "Where do I fit?"

Over time, economic systems came to value efficiency and measurable output. Hours worked and tasks completed became common measures of value. Productivity often took precedence over reflection, and in many settings a person's worth seemed closely linked to visible performance.

As automation takes on more repetitive and predictable work, the nature of labor is changing. When systems manage routine tasks, human effort moves away from repetition and toward interpretation, design, and relationship. This shift raises a larger question about purpose. If survival alone no longer defines work, what gives contribution its meaning?

"Work is not what we do to live. It is how we bring life into what we do." - *Santiago Dagon*

Generation Alpha may approach employment with different expectations. Work may be evaluated not only by compensation, but also by alignment with personal values and broader impact. Contribution could extend beyond individual gain to include social and environmental awareness.

Purpose does not remove responsibility. Bills still need to be paid, and systems remain in place. At the same time, the conversation around work is expanding. As labor evolves, fulfillment may be defined less by productivity and more by the chance to express oneself and take part in meaningful work.

Freedom And The Burden Of Choice

Digital infrastructure has widened access to opportunity. Work can be performed remotely. Skills can be acquired through open platforms. Creative projects can reach audiences without traditional gatekeepers. The barriers that once limited entry into certain fields have, in many cases, lowered.

With this expansion comes complexity. When options multiply, clarity becomes less automatic. The absence of restriction does not guarantee direction. In fact, unlimited pathways can generate hesitation. Decision making becomes a continuous process rather than a one-time commitment.

Generation Alpha is coming of age in a landscape shaped by open possibility. They see adults changing roles, starting new ventures, and pursuing multiple interests at the same time. This signals flexibility. But without a sense of direction, flexibility can become confusing rather than freeing.

"Freedom is not having every door open. It is knowing which one to walk through." - *Santiago Dagon*

Freedom, in this sense, may depend less on access and more on discernment. The ability to concentrate attention, to evaluate priorities, and to commit to a direction becomes central. Choosing a path does not eliminate other possibilities. It gives shape to energy.

As choice continues to expand, the skill of focus may grow in importance. Not every opportunity requires pursuit. In narrowing attention, individuals often discover coherence. Within that coherence, purpose has space to take form.

From Achievement To Alignment

For decades, success was often measured in visible markers. Titles signaled advancement. Income reflected status. Accumulated possessions suggested progress. These indicators formed a public language of accomplishment that was widely understood.

That framework is being reconsidered. While recognition and stability remain important, many individuals now question whether external achievement alone defines fulfillment. Attention is turning inward. The conversation includes not only what has been accomplished, but also whether that accomplishment reflects personal values.

Generation Alpha is observing this recalibration. They see adults reassessing careers, redefining priorities, and speaking more openly about burnout and dissatisfaction. The emphasis appears to be shifting from accumulation to alignment. The question becomes less about how far one has climbed up the career ladder and more about whether the direction matches the person one is becoming.

"The world calls it success. The soul calls it resonance."
- Santiago Dagon

Alignment does not remove difficulty. It does not guarantee ease. It offers coherence. When actions correspond with internal conviction, effort often feels different. The day's work may still demand energy, but it carries a sense of participation rather than compliance.

As cultural definitions of success continue to evolve, alignment may function as an internal compass. It invites reflection about purpose, impact, and identity. In that reflection, achievement is not discarded. It is reexamined through the lens of meaning.

The Rise Of The Purpose Economy

Economic life is showing signs of recalibration. Consumers increasingly ask where products originate, how workers are treated, and what impact a company has beyond revenue. Employees question whether their labor contributes to something constructive. Investment decisions are influenced by environmental and social considerations alongside financial return.

The New Humanity Shift suggests a broader cultural movement. Commerce is no longer evaluated solely by scale or expansion. Reputation now includes transparency, sustainability, and social contribution. Businesses that articulate a clear mission often attract loyalty that extends beyond price comparison.

"Profit without purpose is noise. Purpose without action is silence." - *Santiago Dagon*

Generation Alpha is observing these patterns early. They encounter conversations about ethical sourcing, environmental impact, and corporate accountability in school and media. For them, business enterprise may feel inseparable from responsibility. Innovation and stewardship may be viewed as complementary rather than competing aims.

The idea of a "Purpose Economy" reflects this overlap between meaning and value. Work and organizations are judged not only by efficiency, but by how well they support broader well-being. Whether this approach will become widespread is still uncertain, as markets remain complex. Even so, the growing focus on intention points to an ongoing shift. Commerce may increasingly be seen as part of community life, rather than something separate from it.

Collaboration Over Competition

For much of modern history, achievement was often framed as individual triumph. Innovation was attributed to singular figures. Success stories highlighted personal drive and distinction. Competition was treated as the engine of progress.

That narrative is evolving. Many contemporary breakthroughs emerge from interdisciplinary teams. Scientific advances draw on global networks of researchers. Creative industries blend perspectives from multiple cultures and skill sets. The complexity of modern challenges often exceeds the capacity of any one person.

Generation Alpha is coming of age in a more cooperative environment. Group projects start early, and digital platforms make shared creation a normal part of daily life. Encountering different viewpoints becomes part of solving problems, rather than something to avoid or work around.

"Competition builds walls. Collaboration builds bridges."
- Santiago Dagon

This does not mean competition disappears. It continues to motivate effort and refinement. Collaboration appears increasingly central to sustainable progress. Listening, negotiation, and shared authorship gain prominence alongside individual contribution.

Success within this framework may be measured less by solitary advancement and more by collective impact. Leadership becomes relational. Influence extends through coordination rather than dominance.

As cultural emphasis shifts, the image of success expands. Achievement remains meaningful. What changes is its context. It unfolds within networks of participation rather than isolated ascent.

The Hybrid Life: Work And Well-Being

The separation between workplace and home once felt defined. Commutes marked transition. Offices contained professional roles. Evenings signaled pause. With digital connectivity and remote systems, those lines have blurred. Tasks travel across spaces. Messages arrive outside traditional hours. Work can unfold at a kitchen table or in transit.

This flexibility offers advantages. Parents may adjust schedules around family needs. Individuals can structure days with greater autonomy. Geographic location no longer limits certain professions. Constant accessibility can also erode boundaries. When communication remains uninterrupted, rest may require deliberate effort.

"Rest is not retreat. It is renewal disguised as stillness."
- Santiago Dagon

Generation Alpha is observing adults navigate this integration. They see benefits of adaptability alongside the strain of perpetual engagement. As they enter professional life in the coming decade, their expectations may reflect these observations. Conversations about mental health, burnout, and sustainable pace are already more visible than in previous decades.

Redesigning work to include well-being does not eliminate ambition. It reframes sustainability as essential rather than optional. Structured pauses, realistic workloads, and respect for personal time become elements of effectiveness rather than indulgence.

As hybrid models continue to evolve, balance will likely remain a central theme. The question is not whether work and life intersect, but how intentionally that intersection is shaped. In that shaping, quality of experience may matter as much as productivity itself.

The Spiritual Dimension Of Work

In many earlier societies, labor carried symbolic meaning beyond income. Craftsmanship was often linked to devotion. Farming followed seasonal rhythms that reinforced dependence on land and weather. Making something by hand involved attention that bordered on ritual. Work was not separate from identity or belief. It was integrated into both.

As economies industrialized, emphasis shifted toward scale and speed. Output increased. Efficiency improved. Reverence, however, became less visible in mainstream narratives. Work was frequently framed as competition, advancement, and accumulation.

Recent cultural conversations suggest a renewed interest in purpose. People speak about calling, service, and contribution with language that resembles earlier notions of vocation. Effort is evaluated not only by external reward, but by internal coherence. The quality of attention given to a task begins to matter again.

"When your work becomes service, even the smallest task shines." - *Santiago Dagon*

Generation Alpha may grow up observing this reframing. Acts of care, craftsmanship, and ethical commitment are increasingly visible in public discourse. The idea that work can express values rather than merely secure income is reentering conversation.

Sacredness, in this context, does not require formal ritual. It can appear in the care taken with a project, the respect shown toward colleagues, or the integrity maintained in decision making. When effort is aligned with service, even routine responsibilities take on significance.

As definitions of success continue to evolve, the integration of purpose and practice may influence how this generation approaches labor. Work becomes not only a means of survival or status, but a reflection of intention.

The Redefinition Of Wealth

For generations, wealth was largely defined by visible accumulation. Property, savings, and possessions served as indicators of security and success. Material comfort often signaled stability. The language of prosperity centered on ownership and expansion.

That definition appears to be widening. Many people now talk about wealth as more than money or possessions. It includes having time to be present with family, health that allows daily life to be lived fully, and relationships that last through change. These things function like valuable resources, even though they are not counted or listed in financial records.

"True wealth is what remains when everything that can be bought is gone." - *Santiago Dagon*

Generation Alpha is watching adults rethink what matters. Conversations about work life balance, mental health, and community involvement point to a wider change in priorities. Financial security still matters, but it is increasingly weighed alongside quality of experience.

Experiences often carry more meaning than visible display. Travel, shared projects, and honest conversation become signs of a full life. A sense of inner alignment is beginning to factor into how success is understood.

This redefinition does not dismiss financial responsibility. Resources remain necessary. What seems to be changing is emphasis. Wealth may be understood less as quantity alone and more as alignment between external stability and internal contentment. In that balance, prosperity takes on a broader meaning.

Failure, Resilience, And Redirection

In many traditional models of success, failure was treated as deficiency. Mistakes were hidden. Career changes were questioned. The narrative favored linear ascent without visible detours. Reputation often depends on the appearance of consistency.

Cultural attitudes appear to be shifting. Entrepreneurship, innovation, and creative work have normalized experimentation. Setbacks are discussed more openly. Learning is increasingly framed as iterative rather than final. In this environment, failure becomes less a verdict and more a signal.

"Failure is not falling down. It is refusing to look for the lesson." - *Santiago Dagon*

Generation Alpha has access to many stories of change and reinvention. They see public figures shift careers, start new ventures after loss, and speak openly about setbacks. The idea that direction can change without reducing a person's worth is becoming more visible.

In this context, resilience is not about pushing forward without feeling. It involves adaptation and reflection. It requires looking honestly at what did not work and why. Changing direction becomes part of growth rather than a sign of instability.

As work and identity become more fluid, the ability to pause and reassess may matter more. Change does not cancel earlier effort; it builds on it. In that process, setbacks are reframed as transitions within a longer path of development.

The Future Of Leadership

Leadership has often been associated with hierarchy. Titles conveyed authority. Decisions flowed from the top downward. Distance between leader and team reinforced structure. In many institutions, clarity of command was considered essential to efficiency.

That model is being reconsidered. Contemporary workplaces and communities increasingly value relational skills alongside strategic competence. Listening, transparency, and emotional awareness are discussed as core leadership capacities. Influence appears to grow from credibility and trust rather than position alone.

"The best leaders do not stand in front. They stand beside."
- Santiago Dagon

Generation Alpha is observing these changes early. They encounter mentors who facilitate discussion rather than dictate conclusions. They see organizations highlight collaboration and shared responsibility. Leadership becomes less about control and more about coordination.

Creating environments where people feel seen and secure often leads to stronger participation. When individuals know their perspective is considered, engagement deepens. Authority does not disappear, but it is shown through example rather than distance.

As expectations change, authenticity becomes central to influence. When stated values match lived behavior, credibility grows. In that alignment, leadership moves away from dominance and toward partnership, shaping culture through relationship rather than command.

The Revolution Of Enough

Modern culture often emphasizes expansion. More growth. More visibility. More acquisition. Striving is frequently framed as virtue, and restlessness as motivation. Within this atmosphere, the idea of "enough" can seem counterintuitive.

A different perspective is emerging. Enough does not imply stagnation. It signals discernment. It reflects an awareness that accumulation without reflection can dilute satisfaction. When limits are recognized, attention shifts from comparison to appreciation.

"Enough is not a limit. It is the beginning of peace."
- *Santiago Dagon*

Generation Alpha is hearing conversations about sustainability, burnout, and balance alongside ambition. They see adults slow their pace, question constant acceleration, and rethink what progress means. The idea of "enough" enters these discussions not as giving up, but as a thoughtful adjustment.

Satisfaction and ambition do not have to compete. When goals are shaped by awareness, effort often carries less pressure. Gratitude can exist alongside growth. Recognizing what is sufficient creates room for intention instead of impulse.

As economic and social expectations continue to change, success may be measured not only by achievement, but by contentment as well. In this recalibration, ambition is not removed. It is guided by perspective.

Closing Reflection

The idea of success is expanding. Advancement on its own no longer answers the questions many people are asking. Direction now matters as much as progress. The path taken carries meaning alongside how far one rises.

In this changing landscape, work is less often seen only as obligation. It becomes a way to express values. Contribution is judged not just by scale or visibility, but by how closely intention aligns with action.

"Work is how we sculpt time into meaning. Purpose is the hand that guides the sculpture." - *Santiago Dagon*

Generation Alpha is entering a world where traditional markers of achievement coexist with deeper conversations about fulfillment. They may inherit systems built on competition. They are also witnessing reassessment. Alignment, contribution, and relational impact are gaining visibility.

Redefining success does not eliminate ambition. It reframes it. Achievement without inner correspondence often feels incomplete. When effort reflects conviction, accomplishment carries a different sense of fulfillment.

As this generation shapes its own measures of value, the emphasis may continue to move toward integrity of direction. In that movement, success becomes less about ascent and more about authenticity lived over time.

CHAPTER 14

SPIRITUALITY AND THE INNER WORLD

"The sacred has not disappeared. It has simply changed address, from temples of stone to the space within the human heart." - *Santiago Dagon*

Beneath every cultural shift lies a deeper movement. Technology advances. Economies reorganize. Social norms evolve, but the interior life continues its own unfolding. Questions of meaning, belonging, mortality, and purpose do not disappear in an age of innovation. If anything, they grow more visible.

Generation Alpha is surrounded by stimulation, access, and constant exchange. Information arrives instantly. Opinions circulate rapidly. Identity is shaped in public spaces as much as in private reflection. Within this environment, the inner world does not vanish. It waits.

Spirituality, for this generation, may not follow the patterns of previous eras. Some will inherit structured traditions. Others will explore through personal inquiry, through community, through silence, or through dialogue. The form may vary. The search remains consistent. Generation Alpha children will continue to ask, in their own ways, what is real, what is lasting, and what connects them to something larger than themselves.

The language of spirituality is also broadening. Emotional awareness, mindfulness, compassion, and collective responsibility are entering everyday conversation. Practices once considered specialized are becoming integrated into schools and homes. Reflection is no longer reserved for retreat. It is being woven into ordinary life.

This chapter does not attempt to define spirituality for a generation. It observes how the inner dimension may be developing alongside technological and social change. It considers how awareness, reverence, connection, and meaning are being reframed in a connected world.

The pages that follow are not final statements. They are thoughtful considerations of patterns already emerging. Each section looks at how inner growth may take shape within a culture of speed and saturation.

You are invited to approach these reflections with openness rather than expectation. Notice where they resonate with what you have seen. The purpose is not to forecast certainty, but to explore how the interior life may be evolving and what that evolution could suggest for the future.

The Hunger Beneath The Noise

The contemporary world moves quickly. Information refreshes without pause. Images shift before reflection settles. Attention is pulled in multiple directions at once. For many adults, this acceleration already feels familiar. For Generation Alpha, it is the only pace they have known.

Even within this constant stimulation, another current appears. Moments of withdrawal surface. Generation Alpha children seek spaces where devices are set aside. They gravitate toward activities that slow perception, whether through art, sport, nature, or reflective conversation. These tendencies suggest that the need for inward balance persists regardless of external speed.

Stillness, in this context, is not defined by silence alone. It refers to an internal recalibration. A return to awareness that is not fragmented by competing inputs. As exposure increases, the contrast between stimulation and reflection becomes more visible. Meaning often emerges not from accumulation of information, but from integration.

"When the mind is full, wisdom speaks from stillness."
- Santiago Dagon

Spiritual inquiry for this generation may arise less from formal structure and more from lived experience. When saturation leads to fatigue, questions follow. What truly matters? What endures beyond the scroll? In that questioning, inner life gains relevance.

Rather than beginning with doctrine, exploration may begin with awareness of imbalance. When knowledge feels abundant but understanding feels incomplete, attention turns inward. The search for coherence does not reject the modern world. It seeks orientation within it.

From Religion To Reverence

For much of history, spirituality was closely tied to formal structure. Rituals organized time. Sacred texts guided interpretation. Community gathered around shared belief. These traditions continue to offer meaning and stability for many families today.

At the same time, cultural patterns suggest a widening approach. Some young people engage inherited practices with renewed intention. Others explore spirituality through personal reflection, creative expression, or connection with nature. The shift does not necessarily reject tradition. It reframes how the sacred is encountered.

"Faith begins when we stop defending our version of truth and start listening for its many voices." - *Santiago Dagon*

Generation Alpha is growing up surrounded by many spiritual viewpoints. Exposure to different beliefs and practices is common, which means reverence is less likely to be tied to a single language or tradition. Moments of awe may arise through shared conversation, time in nature, creative expression, or quiet reflection.

Technology also shapes this experience. Meditation apps, streamed services, and online communities allow participation beyond physical place. A Generation Alpha child might listen to a prayer, watch a sunrise video, and then write in a journal. The paths are varied, and meaning often forms through how these experiences are connected rather than through one fixed route.

What appears consistent is the search for authenticity. Sincerity holds influence. Practices that foster reflection, gratitude, or compassion resonate regardless of label. In this context, spirituality becomes less about defending boundaries and more about recognizing meaning wherever it surfaces.

The Inner Landscape

Attention is often directed outward. Screens invite response. Schedules demand movement. Conversation fills space quickly. Within this environment, turning inward can feel unfamiliar. Reflection is not withdrawal. It is engagement with one's own interior experience.

For Generation Alpha children growing up amid constant input, learning to notice thought and emotion without immediate reaction becomes significant. Observing frustration, excitement, or uncertainty without distraction can reveal patterns that otherwise remain hidden. This inward orientation does not eliminate complexity. It clarifies it.

"The soul does not shout. It waits for you to listen."

- Santiago Dagon

Practices that support reflection are increasingly visible in schools and homes. Journaling encourages articulation of feeling. Breath awareness slows physiological response. Time spent alone without digital interruption creates space for integration. These methods are not dramatic. They are structured pauses within activity.

Generation Alpha may come to view such practices as ordinary tools rather than specialized rituals. Through repetition, children can discover that thoughts fluctuate, emotions shift, and identity develops gradually. The inner world is not an adversary to control. It is a landscape to understand.

As reflection becomes more accessible, peace is less framed as something external to pursue and more as an awareness to uncover. The journey inward does not remove engagement with the world. It informs it.

The Spirituality Of Connection

Reflection often begins in solitude. Insight frequently deepens in relationships. Conversation grounded in honesty can alter perspective. Listening without interruption can shift understanding. Acts of compassion create effects that extend beyond the immediate exchange.

For Generation Alpha, spirituality may not be confined to designated spaces. It may surface in ordinary interactions. When a child notices another's distress and responds with care, something interior expands. When forgiveness follows disagreement, a sense of restoration appears.

"Every time we see another person clearly, we glimpse the sacred through their eyes." - *Santiago Dagon*

Connection introduces vulnerability. It requires attention and genuine engagement. In a culture where communication is constant, depth of exchange becomes intentional. Empathy is practiced through patience, through acknowledgment, through restraint in moments of tension.

Small gestures carry meaning. Sitting beside someone without needing to fill silence. Asking a question that invites reflection. Choosing understanding over escalation. These actions do not resemble formal ceremony, but they often shape character more deeply than ritual alone.

As relational awareness grows, spirituality becomes less about separation from daily life and more about engagement within it. In this sense, connection itself becomes formative, shaping the inner world through shared experience.

Technology And The Soul

Digital systems now intersect with nearly every domain of experience, including reflection and emotional awareness. Applications guide breathing exercises. Online communities discuss mental health openly. Recordings of teachers from multiple traditions are available instantly. Access to insight is no longer limited by geography.

At the same time, constant exposure can fragment attention. Notifications interrupt contemplation. Comparison can distort self-perception. The same device that offers instruction can also amplify distraction. The effect often depends on context and intention.

"Even in a digital storm, the soul remembers how to breathe." - *Santiago Dagon*

Generation Alpha will likely view technology as an ordinary part of inner exploration. Guided practices may originate on a screen. Journaling may occur on a keyboard. Dialogue about emotional struggle may unfold in digital forums. These pathways can support awareness when used deliberately.

Discernment becomes central. Not every tool contributes equally to well-being. Recognizing when engagement supports clarity and when it diffuses it is part of developing maturity. The choice of how to engage remains human.

Technology can facilitate access. It does not determine depth. The inner life continues to unfold through attention, reflection, and lived experience, whether or not a device is involved.

The New Mystics

Across history, each generation has included individuals who perceive patterns others overlook. They are not always positioned at the center of attention. Often, they are attentive, reflective, and patient. Their influence grows through insight rather than volume.

Generation Alpha will likely include similar figures. Some may work in technology, shaping systems with ethical awareness. Others may teach, create art, or engage in community leadership. Their distinguishing feature may not be visibility, but depth of perception.

"Visionaries are not those who see farther, but those who see more deeply." - *Santiago Dagon*

Depth does not require display or drama. It often grows from careful attention. The ability to notice subtle shifts in behavior, recognize imbalance in systems, or sense when a conversation has lost its way can shape culture over time.

People with this awareness often act as integrators, bringing reflection into spaces driven by innovation. Their influence may come not from intensity, but from clarity. In environments filled with constant stimulation, steady insight can become a quiet source of guidance.

As this generation matures, such figures may remind others that awareness is not passive. It guides action. Wisdom develops not only through accumulation of information, but through sustained attention to what information reveals.

The Healing Of The Inner Child

Every generation carries forward experiences that were never fully processed. Some stem from pressure to achieve. Others from unspoken grief, comparison, or the pace of modern life. These inheritances are rarely visible at first glance. They surface gradually in habits, expectations, and emotional responses.

Generation Alpha will not be exempt from such influences. Growing up in a highly connected world introduces its own forms of strain. Visibility can intensify self-awareness. Constant feedback can sharpen comparison. At the same time, language around emotional health is more available than in previous decades. Conversations that were once avoided are becoming more open.

"To heal is to let the heart remember it was never truly broken." - *Santiago Dagon*

Healing in this context does not imply correction of defect. It suggests integration. Allowing rest without guilt. Acknowledging feelings without dismissal. Recognizing that imperfection does not negate worth. These gestures cultivate understanding rather than concealment.

Spiritual development may increasingly involve attention to emotional healing. Not through dramatic change, but through steady reflection and reliable support. When Generation Alpha learns that vulnerability does not threaten belonging, resilience often grows stronger.

Reconnecting with early innocence does not mean returning to naivety. It means remembering curiosity, playfulness, and authenticity that may have been pushed aside over time. In that reconnection, growth becomes less about fixing what is broken and more about recognizing what has always remained whole.

The Return Of Awe

Advances in science have expanded visibility in remarkable ways. Telescopes capture distant galaxies. Microscopes reveal intricate cellular systems. Data models illustrate patterns that once remained hidden. Access to such knowledge is no longer confined to laboratories. Generation Alpha children encounter these images in classrooms and on personal devices.

Exposure to complexity does not necessarily reduce wonder. In many cases, it intensifies it. The scale of the universe and the precision of biological systems invite reflection rather than dismissal. Explanation and amazement can coexist.

"Knowledge describes the universe. Wonder allows us to belong to it." - *Santiago Dagon*

Generation Alpha will grow with immediate access to information. Facts can be retrieved in seconds. Still, information does not replace experience. A distant horizon still invites pause. The movement of waves still holds attention. A night sky continues to draw quiet reflection.

Reason and reverence do not have to oppose each other. Careful thinking can deepen appreciation. Observation can encourage humility. As scientific understanding grows, it often reveals new layers of complexity rather than simple answers.

As access to knowledge expands, awe may return not through lack of understanding, but through awareness of scale and connection. In that awareness, belonging moves beyond knowing into participation.

Mindfulness As Modern Faith

In an era defined by distraction, attention is gaining new significance. Mindfulness was once considered a specialized practice is now entering classrooms, offices, and homes.

Exercises that focus on breath, posture, and observation are being introduced as practical tools rather than abstract philosophy.

Mindfulness, in this context, is less about escape and more about orientation. It invites individuals to notice thought patterns, emotional shifts, and physical responses without immediate reaction. Awareness becomes an ongoing stance rather than a temporary exercise.

"Attention is love made visible." - *Santiago Dagon*

Generation Alpha is growing up amidst competing demands for focus. Notifications, media streams, and multitasking create fragmented engagement. The cultivation of sustained attention may become essential rather than optional. When children learn to pause and observe, they often develop greater clarity about their own responses.

Attaining inner peace does not mean stepping away from responsibility or effort. It can appear when everyday activity is met with awareness. When thinking slows enough to be noticed, people have more room to choose how they act. Automatic reactions begin to turn into considered responses.

As mindfulness continues to move into mainstream settings, it may function less as trend and more as stabilizing practice. In a world of rapid input, the capacity to remain attentive could shape how this generation navigates both inner and outer landscapes.

Death, Legacy, And Continuity

Questions about mortality accompany every generation. What has shifted is the way memory is preserved. Voices can be replayed. Images remain stored indefinitely. Messages endure long after they are written. For Generation Alpha, the archive of a life may appear more permanent than in earlier eras.

The preservation of records does not eliminate impermanence. Data can store likeness. It cannot contain lived human relationships with emotions. A photograph captures a moment. It does not carry the full atmosphere in which that moment unfolded.

"What we leave behind is not our image, but the love we awakened in others." - *Santiago Dagon*

Legacy, in this sense, extends beyond documentation. It is carried through influence. Values passed on through example continue in indirect ways. A gesture of kindness can shape another's response years later. A conversation can alter direction in ways unseen at the time.

Generation Alpha will likely navigate both digital memory and lived remembrance. The distinction between archive and impact may become clearer as they mature. What survives most deeply often resides in character shaped by relationship rather than in files stored on servers.

Continuity is experienced through what is practiced and passed on. In that transmission, the thread between generations remains intact, not because everything is recorded, but because something essential is carried forward.

The Soul In The Collective

Spiritual exploration has often been described as a personal journey. Reflection, prayer, study, and contemplation were framed as inward paths. While that dimension remains, there are signs of a parallel movement toward shared experience. Small groups gather to reflect, meditate, discuss, and support one another. Some meet in physical spaces. Others connect through digital platforms that bridge distance.

This collective dimension does not replace individual inquiry. It complements it. When people share insights, language for inner experience expands. When vulnerability is expressed in community, isolation can lessen. Spiritual awareness becomes something practiced in relationships rather than pursued alone.

"Enlightenment is not a destination. It is the moment humanity remembers it is one mind." - *Santiago Dagon*

Generation Alpha has access to global conversations about consciousness, well-being, and purpose. They see discussions that cross cultures and borders, and they hear the idea that inner development contributes to collective health. This perspective is becoming more common in public dialogue.

In this context, spirituality may be experienced as participation in a shared field of awareness. Personal growth shapes how people interact, and those interactions shape community life. As a result, the line between inner experience and outward behavior becomes more open and connected.

As shared reflection becomes more common, the language of awakening may move away from individual achievement and toward collective connection. Personal well-being is increasingly understood as linked to the well-being of others. In that understanding, spirituality becomes less about the Self alone and more about relationships and shared life.

Closing Reflection

Generation Alpha is growing up where rapid innovation meets long-standing tradition. Technology advances quickly, while inherited stories and ideas continue to shape human reflection. They encounter advanced systems alongside teachings that have endured for centuries. Even as the world around them moves fast, inner life still develops at its own pace.

In a time when machines can imitate reasoning and language, one capacity remains uniquely human. Awareness cannot be automated. Attention cannot be handed off. The ability to notice thoughts, recognize emotion, and pause before reacting belongs to lived experience itself.

"The inner world is not a place we visit. It is the home we were never meant to leave." - *Santiago Dagon*

For Generation Alpha, the challenge will not be to avoid complexity, but to stay attentive within it. Pressure will remain. Expectations will continue. Even so, clarity can grow alongside them. When awareness guides action, responses become thoughtful rather than reactive.

Spiritual depth, in this sense, does not pull away from everyday life. It shapes how life is lived. Compassion shows up in ordinary interactions. Reflection supports decision making. Strength is expressed through understanding rather than force.

As this generation matures, their influence may come less from intensity and more from steadiness of perception. In a time of rapid change, the ability to remain conscious may help align inner development with outward progress, allowing both to move forward together.

CHAPTER 15

COMPASSION, EMPATHY, AND GLOBAL LEADERSHIP

**"Leadership without empathy is management of things.
Leadership with empathy is guidance of souls."**
- Santiago Dagon

Leadership is being reshaped by the conditions of a connected world. Decisions no longer affect a single town, country, or continent. Policies, innovations, and cultural movements travel quickly across global borders. In such an environment, authority alone is insufficient. Influence increasingly depends on relational awareness.

Generation Alpha is cradled within this interwoven landscape. They witness global events unfold in real time. They observe communities responding to crisis, celebration, conflict, and recovery across distance. Exposure to shared experience broadens perspective at an early age. Emotional intelligence is not separate from civic life. It is part of it.

Compassion and empathy, once described as personal virtues, are becoming structural necessities. Complex challenges require collaboration among diverse voices. Listening becomes strategic. Understanding becomes practical. Emotional maturity shapes the tone of public discourse as much as policy expertise shapes content.

This chapter explores how relational intelligence may influence leadership in the years ahead. It considers how empathy informs governance, how compassion reshapes commerce, and how cooperation may redefine power. The focus is not on idealism alone, but on observable cultural movement.

The reflections that follow are not definitive pronouncements. They are careful observations of patterns already visible. Each section offers a perspective on how emotional development and global responsibility may intersect in a rapidly evolving society.

You are invited to approach these pages as thoughtful inquiry rather than final judgment. The aim is not to forecast a fixed future, but to examine how compassion and empathy may be shaping the next chapter of leadership in an interconnected world.

The Heart Of A New Kind Of Power

Leadership has traditionally been linked to control. Authority came with titles, decisions moved from the top down, and strength was often measured by visibility and command. In many systems, people had influence because of their place in an organized hierarchy.

As global challenges become more complex, this model of leadership is being reconsidered. Issues like environmental stress, cultural division, and rapid technological change cannot be solved through directive power alone. Addressing them increasingly requires cooperation across borders and viewpoints. In this environment, relational skills become as important as strategy.

Power expressed without empathy can generate compliance, but it rarely sustains trust. Listening, by contrast, invites participation. The ability to recognize emotional undercurrents within communities or institutions can shape more durable responses than assertion alone.

"The true leader does not raise their voice. They raise the strength of everyone around them." - *Santiago Dagon*

Generation Alpha is observing leadership in transition. They witness public figures praised for collaboration as often as for dominance. They encounter discussions about mental health, inclusion, and social responsibility in civic discourse. Influence appears to be shifting from command to connection.

Awareness does not reduce decisiveness. It shapes it. When leaders understand the lived experience of those they serve, policies and initiatives often reflect greater nuance. The capacity to sense collective mood, to respond without escalation, and to maintain composure amid uncertainty may define the emerging style of leadership.

In this recalibration, power is not reduced. It is redirected. Strength becomes relational rather than imposing, shaped by the ability to elevate others rather than overshadow them.

The Empathic Evolution

Empathy is often mistaken for weakness, while playing a stabilizing role in social life. Cooperation has helped communities endure environmental change, conflict, and uncertainty. Awareness of another person's experience builds trust and supports shared resilience.

Generation Alpha is growing up with immediate visibility into global events. Natural disasters, social movements, and cultural celebrations are seen in real time. Children watch how communities respond to loss and recovery across distance. This shared exposure can expand their sense of connection beyond local boundaries.

"Empathy is the nervous system of the human family."
- Santiago Dagon

This expanded awareness carries complexity. Constant visibility into suffering can intensify emotional load. The capacity to care must be accompanied by the capacity to regulate. Without balance, compassion can become depletion rather than strength.

Learning to remain receptive without absorbing every burden may become essential. Empathy does not require constant immersion. It can be expressed through focused action, attentive listening, and sustained commitment to specific causes.

As this generation matures, compassion may evolve into a more structured form of engagement. Feeling deeply and responding wisely are not opposing capacities. Together, they form a pattern of endurance that allows care to remain active rather than exhausted.

The Courage To Feel

In many cultural narratives, strength was equated with restraint. Leaders were expected to maintain composure, suppress doubt, and project certainty. Emotion was often treated as a private matter, separate from public responsibility.

That expectation is being reconsidered. Conversations about mental health, transparency, and authenticity are more visible in professional and civic spaces. Emotional intelligence is increasingly recognized as a component of effective leadership rather than a distraction from it.

"Courage is not the absence of pain. It is the refusal to close the heart." - *Santiago Dagon*

Generation Alpha is observing adults who speak openly about uncertainty and recovery. They see leaders acknowledge mistakes and adjust course. These moments of openness can foster trust. When vulnerability is expressed with integrity, it often invites honesty in return.

The capacity to feel does not eliminate accountability. It strengthens relational bonds. A leader who can admit concern, listen without defensiveness, or extend forgiveness without calculation often creates an atmosphere of psychological safety. In such environments, collaboration deepens.

As emotional awareness becomes more integrated into public life, courage may be defined less by invulnerability and more by attentive engagement. Keeping the heart open in complex situations can shape leadership that is both human and resilient.

The Mirror Of Diversity

Communities today reflect a wide range of cultures, languages, and identities interacting within shared spaces. For Generation Alpha, this plurality is not a distant concept. It is woven into classrooms, neighborhoods, and digital communities. Exposure to varied perspectives becomes part of ordinary experience rather than a rare encounter.

Such visibility invites reinterpretation. Difference can be perceived as complexity rather than contradiction. When children encounter customs and viewpoints unlike their own, they are presented with opportunities to compare, question, and expand understanding. Familiarity grows through repetition of contact.

"Diversity is not what divides us. It is the palette through which compassion paints its masterpiece."
- Santiago Dagon

Recognizing oneself within unfamiliar narratives can shift perception. Shared emotions often bridge cultural distinctions. Joy, loss, aspiration, and uncertainty resonate across context. In that recognition, empathy broadens.

Leadership within diverse environments may rely less on uniformity and more on attentiveness. Curiosity becomes a functional skill. Asking informed questions, acknowledging varied histories, and adapting communication styles can strengthen collaboration.

As Generation Alpha matures in this mosaic, their capacity to navigate difference may influence how institutions and communities evolve. Diversity does not eliminate challenges. It expands the field of perspective from which solutions can emerge.

From Competition To Cooperation

Modern culture has often framed progress as a contest. Rankings, awards, and performance metrics have reinforced the idea that advancement depends on surpassing others. This mindset has fueled innovation, and in doing so has narrowed definitions of success.

Increasingly, complex global challenges require coordination rather than rivalry. Climate response, public health, economic stability, and technological ethics involve multiple stakeholders across borders. No single institution or individual can address these issues in isolation. Cooperation becomes practical rather than idealistic.

"The highest seat at the table is often the one closest to everyone else." - *Santiago Dagon*

Generation Alpha is observing collaborative models early. Group learning, shared platforms, and cross-cultural dialogue are common features of their environment. Influence within such networks depends on listening and integration rather than dominance.

Leadership shaped by cooperation does not eliminate excellence. It situates achievement within collective context. When contributions are aligned toward shared goals, outcomes often extend beyond what individual effort alone could accomplish.

As cultural emphasis continues to shift, the image of success may move from ascent to participation. Structures may resemble circles of coordination rather than ladders of hierarchy. In that configuration, value is distributed across relationships rather than concentrated at a single point.

The Emotional Intelligence Revolution

Technical knowledge remains important in a complex world. Coding, engineering, analytics, and design shape the infrastructure of daily life. Alongside these competencies, another capacity is gaining attention. Emotional awareness is increasingly recognized as central to collaboration and leadership.

For Generation Alpha, emotional awareness begins with noticing feelings in themselves and recognizing them in others. Emotional intelligence goes a step further. It is the ability to use that awareness in real situations, deciding how to respond, handle tension, and move through social spaces shaped by constant interaction and visibility. In a world where emotions are shared quickly and publicly, emotional intelligence becomes the skill that helps awareness turn into steady action rather than reaction.

Understanding one's own reactions, recognizing unspoken tension, and adjusting tone in response to context influence outcomes in ways metrics cannot fully capture. The ability to pause before responding, to interpret feeling as information rather than threat, alters the direction of conversation and decision.

"Intelligence builds the bridge. Emotion decides whether we cross it." - *Santiago Dagon*

Generation Alpha lives in environments where conversations about mental health and interpersonal dynamics are more visible. Schools incorporate social and emotional learning. Workplaces discuss psychological safety. Public discourse includes language about empathy and regulation that was once reserved for private spaces.

When individuals feel acknowledged, participation often deepens. Safety can encourage creativity. Valuation can foster initiative. These patterns suggest that emotional intelligence is not peripheral to effectiveness. It shapes it.

As leadership models evolve, technical mastery may remain foundational. Emotional maturity may determine influence. The capacity to interpret and respond with awareness can transform structures from transactional systems into relational networks. In that transformation, leadership becomes less about command and more about connection.

Compassion In Action

Empathy recognizes another's experience. Compassion extends that recognition into response. It combines awareness with intention. Feeling alone can remain internal. Compassion introduces movement.

In complex societies, responsibility does not rest solely with individuals. Policies, institutions, and systems shape outcomes. When leaders integrate empathy into decision making, priorities often shift. Questions of dignity, access, and fairness gain visibility alongside efficiency and growth.

"Kindness without courage is comfort. Courage without kindness is chaos. Compassion is both."- *Santiago Dagon*

Generation Alpha is observing conversations about restorative justice, inclusive design, and ethical governance at earlier ages. They encounter language about accountability and repair in educational and civic settings. The idea that leadership involves service rather than spectacle is gaining cultural ground.

Compassion in practice may appear in how systems are structured. Does a policy protect the vulnerable? Does an innovation widen opportunity or concentrate advantage? Does a response to conflict aim at resolution or retaliation?

Leadership informed by compassion does not abandon strength. It integrates it. Decisions can remain firm while acknowledging human consequences. In that balance, authority is exercised with awareness of impact.

As expectations evolve, leadership may increasingly be measured not by visibility alone, but by the degree to which dignity is preserved and harm is addressed. In that recalibration, compassion becomes not an accessory to power, but a guiding principle.

The Empathy Economy

Stock markets have traditionally prioritized efficiency, growth, and shareholder return. These measures remain influential. Recent consumer behavior and workforce expectations suggest a parallel shift. Increasingly, people evaluate organizations not only by products or services, but by stated values and visible conduct.

Transparency now travels quickly. Supply chains are examined. Labor practices are discussed publicly. Environmental impact becomes part of brand identity. Trust, once assumed, is now assessed. Companies are observed not only for what they produce, but for how they operate.

"In the future, the richest companies will be the ones that make humanity richer." - *Santiago Dagon*

Generation Alpha exists within this climate of scrutiny and expectation. They will encounter conversations about ethical sourcing, sustainability, and social responsibility in everyday media. For them, the idea that commerce and conscience intersect may feel intuitive.

Fiduciary responsibility is very important in this framework. Financial stability remains necessary for continuity. What appears to be evolving is the understanding that economic success and human well-being need not compete. Organizations can generate revenue while contributing positively to communities and ecosystems.

As this emphasis develops, business may increasingly be viewed as a participant in social life rather than an entity apart from it. The language of impact expands beyond quarterly performance to include long term influence. In that expansion, empathy becomes part of economic calculation rather than an afterthought.

Global Leadership Through Awareness

Public life now takes place in constant exchange. Commentary appears immediately, and reactions often multiply before reflection has time to settle. Attention can be gained quickly, but it can also move on just as fast. In this environment, steadiness stands out.

Leadership in this climate may rely less on volume and more on composure. When conversations intensify, the person who stays attentive can help guide direction without increasing tension. Awareness acts as a point of orientation, slowing reaction and bringing clarity to response.

"Awareness is not the absence of motion. It is what brings clarity to movement." - *Santiago Dagon*

Generation Alpha is observing leaders operate within digital immediacy. They see the consequences of impulsive communication and the value of measured engagement. Calm does not signal passivity. It reflects regulation and perspective.

Influence shaped by sincerity often carries durability. When individuals speak from grounded conviction rather than performance, trust tends to deepen. Spectacle may attract attention. Consistency sustains it.

As leadership evolves in a connected world, sustained awareness may serve as stabilizing force. In moments of rapid change, the capacity to remain attentive can guide collective movement with clarity rather than escalation.

Compassionate Governance

Public leadership has often emphasized efficiency, authority, and ideological clarity. Legislation moved through formal channels shaped by negotiation and debate. While these structures remain essential, the expectations surrounding them are evolving.

Generation Z and soon Generation Alpha are seeing how policies shape daily life in concrete ways. Environmental impact, access to health care, digital privacy, and social equity are discussed openly and often experienced directly. Governance no longer feels distant from personal experience. Its effects are visible in real time.

"Politics without empathy is machinery. Empathy without structure is a dream. The future needs both."

- Santiago Dagon

For Generation Alpha, civic responsibility may involve bringing emotion and structure together. Listening becomes part of leadership. Discussion comes before decision. Policies are judged not only by whether they work on paper, but by how they affect real people.

Balancing different needs is still difficult. Rights and responsibilities overlap. Innovation brings both opportunity and risk. Compassionate governance does not remove disagreement, but it changes how disagreement is handled, with attention to dignity and long-term impact.

As this generation moves into public roles, influence may be shaped by a stronger sense of interdependence. Authority does not come from holding power alone. It is maintained through trust. When leaders see themselves as caretakers rather than owners of responsibility, governance begins to shift from control toward service.

The Education Of The Heart

Compassion does not develop on its own. It grows through example, repetition, and shared experience. Children notice how adults speak to one another, how conflict is handled, and how care shows up in everyday moments. Stories also play a role. Narratives that emphasize fairness, courage, and understanding shape imagination long before abstract ideas are introduced.

"Teach a child to count, and they will know numbers. Teach a child to care, and they will know the universe."
- Santiago Dagon

Educational environments are increasingly acknowledging that intellectual growth and emotional development are intertwined.

Social and emotional learning frameworks are being integrated alongside mathematics and literacy. Students practice recognizing feelings, resolving conflict, and articulating perspective.

This New Humanity Shift does not diminish academic rigor. It expands it. Understanding how to collaborate, regulate response, and communicate respectfully often influences performance across disciplines. When classrooms cultivate psychological safety, participation tends to increase.

Generation Alpha schools will be places where empathy is discussed openly. The ability to interpret emotion, extend respect, and repair misunderstanding may shape their leadership more profoundly than standardized metrics alone.

As these practices become embedded in educational culture, the formation of character Gains visibility. The heart, like the intellect, requires cultivation. When both are engaged, learning becomes more than acquisition of information. It becomes preparation for shared responsibility.

The Legacy Of Kindness

Strength has frequently been associated with intensity, control, or visible dominance. Cultural narratives have often elevated leaders who assert authority decisively and defend position firmly. Within that framework, restraint can be misread as fragility.

Influence expressed without aggression often proves durable. The ability to guide without humiliation, to correct without harm, and to persuade without coercion reflects a disciplined form of strength. It requires regulation, restraint, and clarity of purpose.

"Restraint is not the absence of power. It is power without violence." - *Santiago Dagon*

Generation Alpha is witnessing leadership styles that emphasize dialogue and inclusion alongside decisiveness. They observe how hostility can fracture communities, while respect can stabilize them. The contrast becomes instructive.

Kindness in leadership does not eliminate accountability. It frames it differently. Expectations remain. Standards remain. What changes is the manner in which authority is exercised. When individuals feel respected, participation often increases.

As this generation shapes institutions, sustainability may depend less on force and more on relational credibility. Influence grounded in care tends to endure beyond immediate outcomes. In that endurance, leadership leaves a legacy not of conquest, but of continuity shaped by compassion.

Closing Reflection

Compassion and empathy are no longer peripheral qualities in public life. In a world where decisions ripple quickly across borders, relational awareness becomes foundational. When progress unfolds without regard for human impact, it can destabilize more than it improves. When care informs direction, development gains depth.

"The world does not need more powerful people. It needs more powerful hearts." - *Santiago Dagon*

Generation Alpha will enter adulthood with a strong awareness of global interdependence. From an early age, they see how actions affect systems beyond their immediate environment. In this context, leadership may depend less on forceful momentum and more on careful coordination.

Working alongside communities rather than pushing ahead of them can build trust. Humility can exist alongside confidence. Cooperation may take the place of dominance as a primary form of influence.

If this orientation continues to develop, ideas of strength may shift. Strength may be recognized not in the ability to overpower, but in the capacity to support, protect, and restore. In that shift, leadership becomes less about control and more about stewardship within a shared world.

PART IV

THE FUTURE OF HUMANITY

CHAPTER 16

THE FUTURE OF HUMANITY

"Humanity is not ending. It is remembering."
- Santiago Dagon

Every generation wonders where the human story is heading. Some imagine progress in terms of technology. Others measure it by wealth, stability, or influence. Beneath these markers lies a deeper question: how are we changing, not only in what we build, but in who we are becoming?

Generation Alpha arrives at a pivotal moment. They inherit extraordinary capability. Artificial intelligence accelerates decision making. Global networks dissolve distance. Scientific insight expands daily. At the same time, environmental strain, social division, and spiritual fatigue are visible across cultures. Capacity and consequences now stand side by side.

The New Humanity Shift does not suggest a sudden transformation. It points toward gradual reorientation. A movement from speed toward reflection. From accumulation toward alignment. From dominance toward stewardship. This shift may be less about invention and more about integration.

Less about conquering new frontiers and more about understanding how interconnected we have always been.

Generation Alpha will not bring about this change on their own, but they may carry it more naturally. They are immersed in a world where global awareness is ordinary and emotional language is more accessible. Their development may reflect not a break from previous generations, but a continuation of an evolution that is already in motion.

The sections that follow are not definitive forecasts of what The New Humanity Shift will become. The sections are thoughtful observations of patterns emerging in real time. Each theme considers how awareness, responsibility, and collective identity may develop within a culture defined by connection and acceleration.

As you read, allow space for your own interpretation. Notice what resonates with your lived experiences. Observe how these ideas appear in the children, families, and communities around you. The New Humanity Shift will not affect everyone in identical ways. It will unfold through personal choices, cultural responses, and generational dialogue.

This chapter does not ask you to agree. It invites you to reflect. The future of humanity is not a fixed script. It is a conversation still forming, one in which you already have a voice.

The New Humanity Shift Begins

Every generation inherits a threshold. It receives the world as it is and senses, often intuitively, how it might change.

Generation Alpha arrives at a moment of unusual density. Information surrounds them. Systems respond instantly. Ideas circulate before reflection settles. They are growing up inside acceleration.

And yet, beneath the speed, familiar questions persist.

Who are we becoming?

What does it mean to live well?

Where is the human story moving?

These are not technological questions. They are human ones. They echo across centuries, even as the context transforms. The New Humanity Shift may not begin with invention. It may begin with renewed inquiry.

"When humanity begins asking the right questions again, the future begins to listen." - *Santiago Dagon*

This emerging shift does not reject progress. It reframes it. Innovation alone does not determine direction. Awareness shapes outcome. The tools of this century are powerful. The consciousness guiding them remains decisive.

Generation Alpha stands at the intersection of capacity and choice. Surrounded by advanced systems, they may also rediscover interior clarity. In that rediscovery, the future becomes less about speed and more about orientation.

The New Humanity Shift may not announce itself loudly. It may unfold through a gradual recalibration of values, through attention that deepens rather than fragments. If this generation learns to remain attentive while creating, progress may take on a different tone. Not merely expansion but understanding.

The Age Of Conscious Creation

Creation has accelerated. A concept formed in one corner of the world can circulate globally within hours. Platforms amplify ideas quickly. Collaboration occurs across borders without pause. Generation Alpha is entering a landscape where participation in innovation is more accessible than ever before.

Speed, however, does not guarantee depth. When production outpaces reflection, understanding can fragment. The ability to generate content, design systems, or mobilize movements does not automatically include clarity of direction. Intention becomes as significant as invention.

"We have learned to build everything except peace within ourselves." - *Santiago Dagon*

The New Humanity Shift may depend less on output and more on orientation. As tools become more capable, the inner state of the creator gains influence. Reflection can temper impulse. Awareness can guide ambition.

Generation Alpha is growing up with both extraordinary capacity and visible consequences. They see how innovation can connect and divide, heal and harm. This exposure may foster discernment earlier in life. The question may not be "Can we build it?" but "Should we?"

Conscious creation suggests integration. It brings together imagination and responsibility. It invites pause before proliferation. In this emerging age, maturity may be expressed not through volume of production, but through coherence between intention and outcome.

If such coherence takes root, the most transformative development may not be technological alone. It may be the cultivation of minds capable of aligning creativity with care.

The Shift From Growth To Harmony

For much of the modern era, advancement was equated with expansion. Increased production signaled strength. Faster systems implied efficiency. Accumulation suggested security. Growth became the dominant measure of success across economies and institutions.

Signs of strain have become more visible. Environmental systems respond to overuse. Communities express fatigue under constant acceleration. The natural world operates according to cycles, not perpetual escalation. Human well-being follows similar patterns.

"Harmony is not the end of motion. It is motion in rhythm with life." - *Santiago Dagon*

The New Humanity Shift may involve recalibrating the meaning of progress. Expansion alone cannot remain the sole metric. Balance enters the conversation not as limitation, but as refinement. Sustainability becomes integral rather than optional.

Generation Alpha will have heightened awareness of ecological impact and social interdependence. They will observe both consequences and possibilities. The planet they inherit carries signs of exhaustion. It also demonstrates resilience. Renewal remains possible when direction changes.

Harmony does not halt innovation. It situates it within context. When movement aligns with environmental and human rhythms, development can continue without depletion. In that alignment, progress matures from acceleration into integration.

The Return Of Purpose

Information has become abundant. Answers appear instantly. Data accumulates without effort. Access to facts does not always resolve uncertainty. Many people describe a paradox: knowing more while feeling less oriented.

Purpose operates differently from information. It organizes experience. It helps determine which pursuits deserve attention and which can be set aside. Without it, accumulation can feel directionless. With it, even limited knowledge can feel sufficient.

"Knowledge answers questions. Meaning decides which questions are worth asking." - *Santiago Dagon*

Generation Alpha will have extraordinary cognitive resources. They can retrieve explanations with ease. The challenge may not be scarcity of data, but discernment about its relevance. Understanding requires more than retrieval. It requires interpretation.

The New Humanity Shift may involve rebalancing emphasis. Efficiency and output remain valuable. Beneath them, the search for coherence continues. Generation Alpha children will sense when information lacks context. They ask not only how something works, but why it matters.

In environments defined by speed, the act of pausing gains significance. Reflection allows experience to settle. When movement slows, connections become visible. Through that pause, purpose reenters the conversation, not as abstraction, but as orientation within complexity.

The Rise Of Collective Consciousness

Modern history has often celebrated individual brilliance. Innovation was attributed to singular vision. Breakthroughs were associated with names and titles. Contemporary challenges rarely remain confined to one location. Environmental disruption, public health crises, economic instability, and digital ethics extend beyond borders.

Such complexity invites distributed thinking. Solutions increasingly emerge through networks rather than isolation. Research collaborations span continents. Public conversations unfold across platforms. Responsibility is shared.

"The future of intelligence is not in one mind. It is in many hearts connected by awareness." - *Santiago Dagon*

Generation Alpha will live within a web of interdependence. They will witness global responses to events in real time. A storm in one region prompts concern elsewhere. A cultural loss in one community elicits reflection across distance. Emotional awareness travels quickly.

This phenomenon does not erase individuality. It reframes it. Unity need not imply sameness. It suggests coordinated recognition. When awareness expands beyond immediate surroundings, perspective broadens.

The New Humanity Shift may be characterized less by isolated advancement and more by integrated understanding. As communication links communities more tightly, shared reflection becomes possible. Within that shared space, collective consciousness emerges not as ideology, but as recognition of interconnection.

Beyond Fear And Division

Fear has long influenced collective behavior. It has defined alliances, justified boundaries, and shaped narratives of identity. In many eras, caution toward the unfamiliar was framed as protection. In a connected world, rigid separation becomes difficult to maintain.

Information now crosses borders instantly. Cultural exchange is routine. Economic and environmental systems intertwine. The distance that once sustained isolation has narrowed. Within this proximity, fear often reveals its limits. Defensive posture can stall cooperation when cooperation is required.

"When fear ends, history begins again." - *Santiago Dagon*

Generation Alpha will experience visible diversity and global interdependence. They will encounter multiple perspectives as part of daily experience. Exposure does not eliminate tension.

It can reduce unfamiliarity. Curiosity becomes functional rather than optional.

Choosing understanding over reflexive suspicion does not dismiss difference. It reframes response. Openness allows dialogue where avoidance once prevailed. In that shift, courage is expressed through engagement rather than withdrawal.

The New Humanity Shift may involve recognizing that division cannot resolve shared challenges. When interconnection becomes undeniable, perspective expands. In expanding perspective, fear loses some of its authority, and cooperation gains relevance.

Spiritual Technology

As digital systems grow more capable, the human interior gains new significance. Tools can analyze patterns, generate language, and simulate reasoning. Their role expands daily. The question that follows is not only what machines can do, but how people orient themselves while using them.

Balance between external advancement and internal clarity is becoming increasingly relevant. When innovation accelerates, reflection provides context. Without it, capability can outpace judgment. With it, development gains direction.

"The next great invention will not be a machine. It will be the awakened mind." - *Santiago Dagon*

Generation Alpha will have access to systems that mirror thought and anticipate preference. Living in such proximity to adaptive technology may heighten the need for self-awareness.

Recognizing impulse, intention, and emotional response becomes part of digital literacy.

Practices that cultivate attention and reflection are no longer peripheral. They function as stabilizing capacities. Meditation, journaling, contemplative pause, and intentional dialogue help integrate experience rather than fragment it.

In the unfolding New Humanity Shift, progress may depend not only on technical sophistication, but on interior development. When awareness guides interaction with intelligent systems, humanity remains active participant rather than passive reactor. In that alignment, technology and consciousness evolve together rather than in tension.

The Renewal Of Humanity's Soul

Throughout history, societies have expanded, fractured, rebuilt, and re-examined themselves. Periods of rapid advancement are often followed by reflection. In time, cultures ask not only what has been achieved, but what has been overlooked.

Innovation can transform infrastructure and communication. It does not automatically refine character. When momentum outpaces introspection, imbalance appears. Reflection then becomes necessary, not as retreat, but as recalibration.

"The soul does not evolve by invention. It evolves by remembering." - *Santiago Dagon*

The New Humanity Shift may be understood as such a recalibration. Remembering does not imply regression. It suggests returning to principles that anchor progress: dignity, accountability, and relational awareness. These values are not new. They require renewal.

Generation Alpha will see technological brilliance alongside social strain. They witness efficiency paired with fragmentation. This dual awareness may cultivate discernment.

Restoring consideration in environments that have become transactional. Introducing humility into systems structured around dominance. Reconnecting progress with purpose. These movements do not halt development. They refine it.

As this generation matures, their influence may lie in integration rather than disruption. When conscience accompanies capability, advancement gains coherence. In that coherence, humanity's trajectory becomes less about acceleration alone and more about alignment with enduring principles.

A Planetary Ethic

Ethical systems have often been shaped within borders. Laws reflect national priorities. Cultural norms arise from local history. Yet many contemporary challenges do not remain contained. Climate patterns, migration, supply chains, and digital networks operate across regions and generations.

As interdependence becomes more visible, moral reflection expands. Questions emerge that extend beyond immediate communities. How do present decisions affect distant ecosystems? What responsibilities exist toward future generations? How should human activity account for nonhuman life?

"Morality will evolve from law to love."

- Santiago Dagon

A planetary ethic does not dismiss legislation. It widens its foundation. Compliance may remain necessary. Motivation increasingly includes shared care rather than obligation alone. Survival and compassion no longer appear as opposing aims. Protecting ecological systems, for example, supports both continuity and well-being.

For Generation Alpha environmental awareness will be integrated into education and media. They encounter discussions about sustainability, biodiversity, and global responsibility as part of ordinary discourse. For them, the idea that humanity participates within larger systems may feel intuitive.

The New Humanity Shift may involve recognizing that care is not sentimental. It is structural. When policies and practices reflect interconnectedness, resilience strengthens. A planetary ethic emerges not as abstract ideal, but as practical orientation within an interdependent world.

The Integration Of Opposites

Public discourse has often been framed in binaries. Science contrasted with spirituality. Logic was set against intuition. Individual interest was weighed against collective need. These divisions simplified complexity. They also narrowed possibilities.

In a connected and rapidly evolving world, rigid separation becomes less sustainable. Scientific inquiry can deepen spiritual reflection. Intuition can inform analysis. Personal fulfillment can coexist with communal responsibility. The categories that once seemed incompatible reveal areas of overlap.

"Opposites are not enemies. They are mirrors showing us where balance begins." - *Santiago Dagon*

Generation Alpha is growing up in blended frameworks. A student may study neuroscience in the morning and practice mindfulness in the afternoon. Technology developers discuss ethics alongside engineering. Entrepreneurs reference well-being alongside profit.

Maturity in this context involves holding tension without forcing premature resolution. Integration requires discernment. It acknowledges differences while seeking coherence.

The New Humanity Shift may be characterized not by dominance of one perspective over another, but by synthesis. When reason and reflection inform one another, understanding broadens. When individuality and interdependence are recognized as complementary, social structures stabilize.

In that integration, wisdom emerges not from victory within debate, but from alignment across contrasts.

The Future Of Love

Love has often been framed as feeling. Romance, affection, attachment. While these dimensions remain important, cultural language around love is widening. Increasingly, it is described not only as emotion, but as orientation.

When awareness guides perception, connection deepens. Seeing another person clearly, acknowledging shared vulnerability, and acting with regard for consequence reflect love in practice rather than in sentiment alone. It becomes visible in structure as well as in relationships.

"The future of love is awareness." - *Santiago Dagon*

Generation Alpha is growing up with conversations about inclusion, dignity, and mutual responsibility. They observe how tone influences dialogue and how small choices affect community climate. Love, in this context, may extend beyond private experience into public design.

It can appear in how systems are built, how policies consider impact, and how strangers are addressed. It emerges in restraint as much as in expression. Responsibility becomes part of affection.

The New Humanity Shift may involve recognizing that love is not limited to intensity of feeling. It is reflected in consistency of action. When awareness shapes interaction, connection is sustained not only by emotion, but by intention.

Humanity's Next Horizon

The coming decades are unlikely to unfold without strain. Inequality persists. Environmental systems require repair. Technological acceleration introduces both promise and risk. Uncertainty will remain part of the landscape.

Difficulty does not prevent development. It often clarifies it. Within challenge, values surface. Communities reveal what they are willing to protect, revise, or rebuild. In moments of tension, priorities become visible.

"The destiny of the species is written in the tenderness of its next generation." - *Santiago Dagon*

Generation Alpha will not step into a completed narrative. They will inherit complexity alongside possibility. The New Humanity Shift does not suggest utopia. It suggests orientation. A movement toward integrating capability with conscience.

Evolution, in this sense, may not be measured solely by innovation or dominance. It may be reflected in relational maturity. How wide can care extend? How can dignity be consistently upheld? How intentionally can power be exercised?

Scaling kindness does not imply sentimentality. It implies structure. When empathy informs policy, commerce, education, and leadership, it moves from personal virtue to collective norm.

The horizon ahead remains open. Within its uncertainty lies capacity. If this generation carries forward awareness and responsibility together, the measure of progress may shift from accumulation to alignment, from speed to coherence, from power to stewardship.

Closing Reflection

The future of humanity is not waiting somewhere beyond reach. It unfolds in ordinary decisions, in small recalibrations of thought and response. Evolution does not always announce itself through spectacle. It often advances through recognition.

Every time empathy is chosen over indifference, something begins to change. Each time attention interrupts distraction, perspective widens. Each time compassion guides restraint rather than control, direction changes. The arc of the human story is shaped in these moments.

"The end of evolution is not perfection. It is awareness."
- Santiago Dagon

Generation Alpha will not step into a world in need of saviors. They will step into a world in need of integration. Their influence may lie not in dramatic rescue, but in gradual reorientation. A reminder that progress without consciousness fractures, while progress guided by care coheres.

The New Humanity Shift may unfold not through revolution alone, but through remembrance. Remembering interdependence. Remembering dignity. Remembering that awareness anchors action.

In that remembering, a new generation does not erase what came before. It builds upon it with greater clarity. The measure of advancement may no longer rest solely on speed or scale, but on the depth of connection that accompanies it.

CONCLUSION

THE NEW HUMANITY SHIFT

"Every generation is born into a different sky. The Generation Alpha will be the first to see the whole horizon, and remember that it was never divided." - *Santiago Dagon*

The future rarely announces itself. It arrives through ordinary moments that carry unexpected significance. A child asks a sincere question and waits for an answer that feels real. A family shares a meal without urgency. Someone pauses before reacting and notices what is already here. These moments do not look like transformation. They open a deeper register of experience. The next chapter of humanity begins there.

Generation Alpha carries a long inheritance. Within them live the echoes of earlier eras, the aspirations that lifted civilizations forward, the wounds that shaped caution, the questions that never fully disappeared. They are not stepping into a world detached from the past. They are continuing an ancient story that is learning a different rhythm. Tools have advanced quickly. Human understanding is beginning to follow.

"The future does not arrive from the distance. It blossoms within the moment we begin to see." - *Santiago Dagon*

Change has never moved through sudden leaps. It unfolds through recognition. Through small shifts in attention. Through young people who sense the world differently and respond with curiosity rather than certainty. Generation Alpha will shape what comes next not only through what they invent, but through how they interpret meaning. Their influence will emerge through empathy, imagination, and the way they reduce harm by understanding complexity rather than denying it.

Progress without awareness loses direction. Improvement without care loses depth. Human development begins to be measured less by reach and more by restraint. Technology widens access. Understanding shapes how that access is used. In an age defined by speed, the capacity to pause becomes a form of intelligence.

"To move quickly is not to advance. To awaken is to arrive."
- *Santiago Dagon*

The story unfolding ahead is not one of machines overtaking humanity. It is the story of humanity recognizing itself again. Behind every invention sits a longing to understand, to express, to connect. Knowledge disconnected from responsibility collapses. Creation without conscience empties itself. The work of this era is not to reject what humans build, but to infuse it with the understanding that gave rise to it.

Somewhere, a child may be assembling something new. A game. A melody. A sentence. A small object shaped by curiosity and hope. They may not realize it. They are participating in a much older unfolding. Skill develops through their hands. Meaning develops through their questions.

"Every new generation is the soul's reminder that creation has never stopped." - *Santiago Dagon*

The future of humanity will not be shaped only in laboratories or councils. It will take form through daily choices. How people speak. How they listen. What they notice when nothing demands attention. Generation Alpha does not replace those who came before them. They continue the line. They reflect back on what earlier generations may have forgotten how to see.

When they one day look back on this period, they may not focus on uncertainty or strain. They may recognize a turning. A gradual reorientation in which humanity shifted from reaction toward understanding. History is not shaped by crisis alone. It is shaped by the desire to remain attentive, to remain caring, to remain aware of what sustains life.

"There is no final dawn, only the continuing of dawn through those who choose to remember." - *Santiago Dagon*

What happens next will not be determined only by the technologies humanity creates, but by the awareness brought to creating them. Invention alone is no longer enough. The way people reflect on their impact, their intentions, and their responsibility to one another now matters just as much.

In this understanding, the Earth is no longer treated as a passive stage where human progress simply plays out. It is recognized as a living system that humans exist within and depend upon. Likewise, other people are no longer viewed primarily through labels, roles, or divisions. They are understood as fellow participants in a shared human journey, shaping and being shaped by the same unfolding future.

Final Reflection

"The journey of humanity is not from darkness to dawn, but from forgetting to remembering. The Generation Alpha will not change what we are. They will remind us of what we have always been."

APPENDIX A

GENERATION TIMELINE

"Each generation is a verse in the same unfinished song. Together, they compose the rhythm of humanity."
- Santiago Dagon

This timeline is not a chart of dates, but a story of lives. Each generation shaped the one that followed. Each carried lessons forward, sometimes clearly and sometimes in silence. What we inherit is not only history, but the emotional memory of those who walked before us.

The Lost Generation

Born 1883–1900

Defining events: World War I, the Industrial Age, early modernism

Traits: Disillusioned, artistic, searching for meaning after profound upheaval

Legacy: They revealed the emotional cost of progress and reminded the world that survival is different from healing.

"They learned that survival is not enough; the soul must also recover."

The Greatest Generation

Born 1901–1927

Defining events: The Great Depression, World War II, early mass media

Traits: Resilient, disciplined, community-minded, stable

Legacy: They rebuilt society through service, sacrifice, and shared responsibility. Much of the modern world rests on their resilient strength.

"They did not inherit peace. They built it, one choice at a time."

The Silent Generation

Born 1928–1945

Defining events: Post-war recovery, rise of television, early civil rights movement.

Traits: Modest, thoughtful, loyal, pragmatic

Legacy: They steadied families and institutions during transition and laid the groundwork for cultural shifts that would reshape society.

"They whispered their wisdom and the world mistook it for silence."

Baby Boomers

Born 1946–1964

Defining events: Postwar prosperity, space race, Vietnam War, cultural revolutions

Traits: Idealistic, driven, expressive, transformative

Legacy: They expanded personal freedom, reshaped politics, and culture, and helped build the global communication systems we now take for granted.

"They traded conformity for consciousness and called it freedom."

Generation X

Born 1965–1980

Defining events: Cold War shifts, personal computing, changing economies

Traits: Independent, skeptical, adaptable, resourceful

Legacy: They bridged the analog and digital eras, carrying the memory of both. They learned to stand between worlds and move through uncertainty with steadiness.

"They learned to navigation in the space between revolution and reflection."

Millennials

Born 1981–1996

Defining events: Internet expansion, 9/11, social media, global recession

Traits: Purpose-driven, collaborative, inventive, socially aware

Legacy: They brought empathy into public conversation, challenged outdated systems, and normalized openness about mental health and diversity.

"They taught the world that meaning matters more than material."

Generation Z

Born 1997–2012

Defining events: Smartphones, streaming, climate urgency, political polarization

Traits: Hyperconnected, expressive, justice-oriented, vulnerable yet courageous

Legacy: They turned digital identity into activism, demanded honesty, and began redefining truth through sincerity rather than certainty.

"They questioned everything and found truth not in certainty but in sincerity."

Generation Alpha

Born 2013–2025

Defining events: Artificial intelligence, global connectivity, post-pandemic society, virtual learning

Traits: Tech-fluent, emotionally intuitive, globally aware, creatively unafraid

Legacy: They are the first generation born inside continuous connection. Their role will be to weave intelligence and empathy into a single way of being.

"They will not inherit the Earth. They will awaken it."

A Glimpse Beyond

A new era Generation Beta will rise as Alpha reaches adulthood. We can already sense its outline in the growing awareness of environmental care, shared intelligence, and collective well-being.

If the 20th century belonged to progress and the 21st to connection, the coming age may belong to consciousness itself; a time when humanity learns to see as one without losing the beauty of individual experience.

"The timeline is not linear. It is a spiral. Each generation circles closer to remembering the whole."

- Santiago Dagon

ACKNOWLEDGEMENTS

"Every generation is a continuation of one awakening. What changes is only the rhythm of its remembering."
- Santiago Dagon

This book came together through many hands and many perspectives. While only two names appear on the cover, the ideas within were informed, supported, and strengthened by the insight and encouragement of many others.

To the researchers and thinkers whose work helped illuminate the patterns of this emerging generation, we are grateful. Your curiosity and rigor gave this project its grounding.

To the Alpha children, whose questions and imagination inspired every chapter, this book belongs to you. You remind us that humanity continues to expand its capacity for awareness and care.

To those who came before us, whose effort and vision shaped the path we now walk, your influence remains alive in these pages.

"To walk beyond time is not to escape it, but to see that every moment is already whole." *- Santiago Dagon*

May this gratitude serve as a reminder that understanding grows through connection, and that each generation helps the next to see more clearly.

ABOUT AUTHORS

Soren Fielding is a writer and cultural observer whose work centers on awareness, emotional development, and the quiet forces that shape identity in modern life. Drawing from contemplative traditions, modern psychology, and social observation, he explores how attention, reflection, and ethical clarity influence both personal growth and collective culture. His contribution brings a steady, integrative perspective to questions of meaning, responsibility, and inner coherence in an age of speed.

Nicholas J. Matyas is an American writer, educator, and researcher whose work focuses on the future of human awareness, human development, and the inner life that shapes every generation. His writing brings together psychology, spirituality, and emerging research on Generation Alpha to explore how young minds form meaning in a world of accelerating change.

Santiago Dagon is the contemplative voice through which Nicholas expresses the deeper questions underlying his research. Writing under this pen name allows him to speak from a reflective register, where insight becomes story and wisdom unfolds through conversation. Santiago represents the belief that awareness grows when we slow down, listen carefully, and meet life with compassion.

Together, Nicholas J. Matyas, Soren Fielding, and Santiago Dagon write from complementary vantage points. The researcher, the contemplative, and the observer converge to offer a multidimensional view of Generation Alpha. Their shared work invites readers to understand this generation not only through data and trends, but through depth, presence, and lived experience.

DISCOVERY WALKABOUT PRESS

Discovery Walkabout Press was founded on a simple belief: reflection is not a retreat from life, but a deeper way of living it.

Our mission is to create thoughtful media that nurture awareness, emotional intelligence, and understanding across generations. We publish books, articles, reflective guides, modern parables, contemplative workbooks, and seminars that invite readers to rediscover peace, purpose, curiosity, and meaningful connection. We seek work that helps people live more consciously, love more honestly, and recognize the extraordinary within everyday life.

Each title published under Discovery Walkabout Press carries a shared philosophy: learning begins in stillness, wisdom grows through relationship, and creativity expands when the mind is clear. We support projects that bridge the spiritual and the practical, encouraging readers to walk thoughtfully through their questions rather than rush toward quick conclusions.

At its heart, Discovery Walkabout Press is committed to mindful storytelling. We value depth over noise, clarity over reaction, and conversation over certainty. Our work explores modern culture, relationships, inner development, and the human search for meaning.

As a publishing house and creative development studio, we welcome collaboration with new and established authors, storytellers, researchers, and educators who share this spirit. If you are developing a manuscript, reflective project, or cultural inquiry that aligns with our values, we invite you to contact us. Growth happens in dialogue, and we believe meaningful work is strengthened through partnership.

To learn more about our current titles and collaborative opportunities, visit: https://discoverywalkabout.com

"We do not find truth by running faster. We find it by learning how to walk with wonder."- *Santiago Dagon*